My First Year in Television

Other Books in the First Year Career Series
Published by Walker and Company

The First Year of Teaching
Edited by Pearl Rock Kane

My First Year as a Doctor
Edited by Melissa Ramsdell

My First Year as a Lawyer
Edited by Mark Simenhoff

My First Year in Book Publishing
Edited by Lisa Healy

My First Year in Journalism
Edited by Dianne Selditch

MY FIRST YEAR IN TELEVISION

REAL-WORLD STORIES FROM AMERICA'S TV PROFESSIONALS

Edited by

L. CAROL RITCHIE

WALKER AND COMPANY
NEW YORK

Copyright © 1995 by L. Carol Ritchie

All rights reserved. No part of this book may be reproduced or transmitted in any form or by any means, electronic or mechanical, including photocopying, recording, or by any information storage and retrieval system, without permission in writing from the Publisher.

First published in the United States of America in 1995 by Walker Publishing Company, Inc.

Published simultaneously in Canada by Thomas Allen & Son Canada, Limited, Markham, Ontario

Library of Congress Cataloging-in-Publication Data
My first year in television : real-world stories from America's TV professionals / edited by L. Carol Ritchie.
    p. cm.
Includes index.
ISBN 0-8027-7424-5 (pbk.)
1. Television broadcasting—United States—Anecdotes.
I. Ritchie, L. Carol.
PN1992.3.U5M9   1995
791.45′0973—dc20   95-9684
CIP

Book design by Glen M. Edelstein

Printed in the United States of America

2 4 6 8 10 9 7 5 3 1

For Peter

Contents

FOREWORD *Howard A. Myrick* — ix

ACKNOWLEDGMENTS — xiii

INTRODUCTION *L. Carol Ritchie* — xv

1. Confessions of a Former Script Ripper *Kevin Vineys* — 1
2. The Case of the Creepy Mentor *Jason Walker* — 11
3. Finessing the Art of Chyron *Cindy Nelson* — 21
4. The Value of a Long List of Names
   Mia Freund Walker — 28
5. Cosell Wore Sunglasses *Peter Mehlman* — 36
6. People Skills and Passion *Deb McDermott* — 42
7. Why Is the Bird Up on the Router Switch? *Sara Just* — 52
8. As Much Pizza as We Could Eat *George Flanigen* — 60

9. Putting Emotions on Hold *Sherry Margolis*		69
10. The Scriptless Weather Girl *Laura Faber*		76
11. The Chair Behind the Anchor's Chair *Alison Craiglow*		85
12. A One-Man Band in Fairbanks *Kelly Schnell Huotari*		91
BIBLIOGRAPHY		103
INDEX		105

Foreword

Each academic year, in the radio, television, and film department that I head at Temple University in Philadelphia, there are two occasions when I expect to see identical expressions on the faces of two different groups of students. The occasions are orientation and graduation. The students in the first instance are entering freshmen; in the second instance, they are graduating seniors. Although the two groups of students may differ in their dress, ages, and in some other attributes, they all have the same look in their eyes: a unique combination of joy and expectation, tinged with a noticeable amount of fear and anxiety.

The newly admitted freshmen are alive with the possibilities the next years hold for them. Yet they wonder, Do I have what it takes to succeed in this academic program? Was it wise of me to choose television as my major? Then comes the heart-stopping question, "What will I do after graduation?"

The graduating seniors are joyous because they have just finished a grueling four years of academic and professional training—and because they have accomplished more than they ever thought they could. Yet they are uneasy and more than a bit nervous about their futures. Individually, they ponder, "What does this next year hold for me? Have I made the right career decision? Wouldn't my future be more assured if I'd majored in accounting?"

The concern about career prospects and future employability is especially acute for those who are unaware (a forgivable condition among freshmen) or have not learned (an unlikely state for graduating seniors) what a dynamic career they have chosen. It is a field that is constantly changing and growing, especially when one looks at it from a broader view—that is, from a *telecommunications* perspective. This is the global view, encompassing the convergence of traditional technologies like broadcasting with newer and emerging technologies like computers, interactive video, and fiber optics; together, these technologies are ushering in the much-touted five-hundred-channel information-on-demand industry. This is the coming state of affairs that is called, euphemistically, the "information superhighway." This is the world whose promises and potentials are headlined in the *Wall Street Journal,* the entertainment sections of daily newspapers, and whose stories are hyped on the covers of major newsmagazines.

This is the world that already exists for our video-game-playing children, telemedicine-practicing doctors, picture-phone subscribers, home-shopping-network consumers, and our video-on-demand technophiles of every stripe. And this is the world that will develop an increasingly voracious appetite for programming. Television and its offshoots are career fields that will always need program producers, writers, directors, communication researchers, facility owners, managers, telecommunications policy experts. Fortunately, we have a host of highly educated people who will be graduating from radio, television, and film departments and their evolving telecommunications programs.

This world will also present options that were previously unthinkable. Low-cost, user-friendly video and computer equipment and other equipment will be so technically advanced that we shall have video equivalents of today's desktop publishing. An era is evolving, already, that will facilitate a new breed of independent producers, information developers, and program suppliers, many of whom will create their own jobs—their own careers!

While looking into the eyes of my young charges, I have tried to give them antianxiety messages. My intent has been to launch them into the world of television with confidence—ready to face the extraordinary challenges and rewards, expected disappointments and unexpected pleasures that they shall certainly encounter, especially in those first few years. Until now, I have had to improvise, drawing bits and pieces from my own life experiences and from anecdotes passed on to me in letters and telephone calls from my former students. How often I have wished for a collection of first-person stories from a wide variety of graduates that I might share with my audiences. Stories full of compassion, humor, and honesty, told by someone other than myself—by someone with no vested interest in recruiting new students or in justifying the time, energy, and expense incurred by graduating seniors.

This volume, *My First Year in Television*, accomplishes just that. The twelve stories that follow are told from the heart—free of academic jargon and puffery—and filled with indispensable information on "what it's really like out here"!

—Howard A. Myrick,
Professor and Chair,
Department of Radio-Television-Film,
Temple University, Philadelphia

Acknowledgments

I'd like to thank the professionals in this book who delved into their pasts and graciously took the time to tell me—and you—their stories. They relived some of their worst mistakes and minor triumphs and re-created their impressions of their first, most uncertain year. Television people know how to tell a good story, and for that I am grateful.

Introduction

After poring over the details of the first year on the job for twelve now successful professionals, several things are abundantly clear:

- Most would never, ever want to go through it again.
- Most would also say, now, that it was more than worth the trouble.
- To get beyond entry level, you must be extremely energetic, able to work flexible hours, and willing to relocate to the far ends of the map.
- Few businesses are harder to break into. There seems to be a bottomless supply of young graduates willing to do menial work for little pay. But the lesson of "My First Year in Television" is that it can be done—that there will be a place for you if you look hard and take a few risks and believe that you have something to offer once you get there.

The people in this book got their jobs by talking to everyone they knew with even a remote connection to the industry, and if they didn't know anyone, they introduced themselves. Then they looked creatively at any opportunity that presented itself. Mia Freund Walker got a job as a secretary at a Boston network affiliate. Cindy Nelson couldn't get an interview with a news director, so she called him on a lark and told him, stretching the truth a bit, that she would be in town only a few days. George Flanigen found out about the television business through the well-connected father of a high school friend, who helped him get a few informational interviews. Kelly Schnell Huotari introduced herself to local station producers, who told her that she could get an entry-level job without a broadcast journalism degree.

The brutal truth is, you need experience to get a job in television, and you need a job to get experience. But there are nooks and crannies—sometimes the merest toeholds—that are open to pure beginners. They may involve the meanest of tasks: photocopying for "Nightline," typing and filing for CNN, ordering pizza for the video crew on an independent production. But those jobs can give a close-up view of what the industry offers, and what it takes to get the job done.

Even those with good college internships have to sacrifice, as Laura Faber discovered, feverishly studying a map so she wouldn't make any mistakes on her tryout for "weather girl." But the job is only as much as its occupant can make of it. Though she yearned for hard news, Faber delivered the weather as if nothing were more important, and learned on-camera skills that would serve her well later. Kevin Vineys's biggest challenge on his first job at CNN was handing the right script to the right person, but he spent some time off watching field crews and satellite desk staff do the challenging jobs he was more interested in. Alison Craiglow answered phones at ABC News, but she did it in the middle of the newsroom, and learned much through osmosis.

A job in television is not free of dreary routine and difficult days. But television can offer a career unlike any other, as these people survived to tell. Most mention the teamwork, the tight deadlines, the sense of a mission. Many had the naive idea going in that the work would be glamorous; now that they've been through the most difficult year, that idea has matured into the realistic belief that there's no better way to see the world.

1

Confessions of a Former Script Ripper

 KEVIN VINEYS

As a general assignment reporter at the *Bay City Times* in Bay City, Michigan, in 1989 I covered all kinds of things, everything from murders to features on retiring bus drivers. Some of these stories were less than great—I don't want to say they were humiliating, but they were sometimes embarrassing to work on. It was embarrassing, for instance, when I tried to glean some amusing anecdotes from one county bus driver, who, after twenty-five years behind the wheel, claimed that nothing funny had ever happened to him. I'll always remember that as one of the low points of working in print journalism.

But several months earlier, before I left graduate school, I had sent a letter and an application to the Cable News Network (CNN). My goal was to enter CNN's VJ, or video journalist, program. When I heard nothing from the network, I accepted a position at the *Bay City Times*. About four or five months after I'd started there, I got a call from somebody in CNN's human resources department. She said CNN was interested, and they wanted to interview me over the phone for a possible job. She said she would call back sometime in the next several weeks.

I waited and waited and waited, and four or five weeks later they called and we had the phone interview. It was fairly brief—"What are you doing now? What are your interests? Name the three top stories in news today"—almost like a quiz. The interview lasted about twenty to thirty minutes. A couple of days after that they called back and said, "We're interested in having you work for us. Let us know by tomorrow if you're interested in the job; we need you in two weeks." The quick decision time was no problem: I agonized over the decision for about an hour and a half, without consulting anyone. I had really enjoyed television in graduate school, and I thought, "Geez—CNN; this is really getting a foot in the door." Plus I wasn't sure exactly what my future would've been at the *Bay City Times*; the city hall reporter was leaving, but I didn't think I had much of a chance at getting that beat. The opportunity at CNN sounded like a sure bet—my phone interviewer was talking to me about benefit plans and dental plans and free Braves tickets. I called back, breathlessly, a couple hours later and said, "Yeah, I'm really interested. Let's do it." That day I gave my notice at the *Times*.

The following weekend I road-tripped the sixteen hours to Atlanta by Ford Pinto and looked for a place to live. I found a place, came back to Michigan to put my things in order, moved down there, and started work. CNN had a big orientation day, and all the new hires went on a tour through the newsroom. It was an incredible experience for me; it's hard to describe my excitement. I felt as if I'd arrived: This was *network news*, and I was going to be part of this whole enterprise! In TV journalism, I felt a real energy that I'd never experienced in print journalism.

Participants in the VJ program are hired for one of two tracks: the technical track (for people with a technical background or who aspire to be tape editors or directors) or the editorial track. The technical VJs ran the cameras and directed "traffic" on the studio floor. I was hired on the editorial track: With my editorial background, I was put to work as a "script ripper."

The script rippers are stationed in a hallway between the newsroom and the studio. In the hallway are two printers, a table with some chairs, and an open area for hanging out and managing the scripts.

The scripts printed out on bulky strips of paper with carbons in between, seven copies of each page. The script ripper's job is to pull the scripts off the printer, pull out the carbons, divvy up each page into its own pile by color, and then arrange them all in numerical order and then run all these little piles into the control room (part of the studio) and give them to the people who need them: the producer, the director, the anchor, and so forth. That's half the job. The other half of the job is running the teleprompter for the anchor.

Operating the teleprompter is pretty cool for about three or four weeks, until you master the job. Then it becomes sort of rote. I was working from five in the morning to three in the afternoon—and on that shift you have a lot of back-to-back news shows. There's not a lot of video, there aren't a lot of news packages—stories with a reporter and video in the field, as opposed to just the anchor reading with background video—but there is a lot of reading on camera. Everything's done at the last minute; you're literally running scripts to various people—it can be very physically demanding. Sometimes you must take care to hand scripts up to the anchor in such a way that you don't appear on camera. On rare occasions, you forget yourself and end up on TV. Fortunately, I never did that, but other people did, and they would sometimes bump into each other or bump into the camera.

At CNN, after working on the VJ job for a while, you get

promoted to the next job, then the next job, and so on. Each time you get a raise and different duties, and you're learning more about television. At the time I didn't think I was learning very much. But I'll never forget how exciting it was to watch live shots from the San Francisco earthquake, which happened right before I got there. We were also covering the trial of Zsa Zsa Gabor for slapping a policeman, and as a journalist, I thought, "What a waste, using all this live time for a celebrity trial." But I found out our ratings were really high, and that people wanted to see this kind of stuff. As script rippers we read the scripts and sometimes we had to correct errors—we weren't copyediting by any stretch—but we learned which anchors were good anchors and which were not. Some cannot function without their script in hand; others are so good at ad libbing that their presentation bears no resemblance to the original script.

The job gets very mundane very quickly. Part of the reason is you're at the bottom of the heap, and as the saying goes, "Shit flows downhill." There were a lot of things that VJs got blamed for—sometimes it was their fault, sometimes not. I made a few egregious errors while I was a VJ, errors that were miscommunications or just plain screwups. The worst mistake of my first year was when I gave one of the anchors the wrong color script. When there are two anchors on air, the anchor who's reading copy on air gets the white copy, and the anchor who's not reading gets a peach copy, so each anchor has a bunch of white scripts and a bunch of peach strips, all mixed together. The anchor is also supposed to look for his or her name at the top of the script so it's apparent which part belongs to which anchor. I mixed the scripts around by accident so that one of the anchors had the wrong color script. An anchor *should* be following along on the teleprompter, even when not reading on camera—that's what an alert anchor does. This anchor was not very alert, and after her coanchor read his story, she wound up reading what the other anchor had just read. Afterward I was blamed, and I apologized. She had it worse than me: She was the one on the air, and her mistake couldn't be forgotten; my mistake didn't show and could be forgotten, but I felt bad and embarrassed. Those kind of things happen a lot—much more than they should.

Many VJs tend to feel alienated from the rest of the network staff because few people talk to them. As noted, they sit in a hallway (through which everyone has to pass to get to the studio, the control room, and the rest of the rooms, for that matter), but no one ever has time to chat. Producers and directors are too busy, stopping only to pick up scripts on their way to the control room, lingering afterward only if there was a problem with the scripts. Writers and copy editors come through on their way to relieve themselves, but then hurry back to their posts. A few technical people linger during their down time, but for the most part, the only people VJs get to know during those months are other VJs.

Several of my coworkers used to take personal offense that producers didn't take the time to learn their names. We were known only as "prompter" when the producer called to tell us about a script page-change (stories are frequently shuffled around during the newscast). "She doesn't even know who we are," sniffed my teleprompter assistant (her job was to arrange the scripts on the little conveyor belt that ran under the teleprompter camera; my job was to run the belt at the anchor's reading speed). But the longer I worked at CNN, the more I realized that so many people are involved with each newscast, it's almost impossible to know all of them.

It's also extremely intimidating to go up and introduce yourself to people in the newsroom, mostly because everyone seems so busy all the time, and besides, you're new around here and don't know who's who. Of course, those people who *do* take the initiative and introduce themselves around, ask questions, get themselves known, often are branded as ass kissers by their peers. The rest just keep their heads down and do their jobs, waiting to get to the next step on the company ladder.

VJs *were* promoted purely on the basis of seniority (now they must also pass a news quiz)—unless someone's performance is really awful; the job of script ripper is so simple there's not much to be bad at. The next position is a job known as "tape logger." It's officially called "tape production coordinator"—a lofty title that gives the impression the job isn't too menial. (In actuality, when I was hired, I was told how menial the first jobs are: "Your duties will be the following . . ." I replied, "Oh, great! I'll sweep the floors to work at CNN!") The tape loggers maintain the short-term videotape library, where all the videos and all the voiceovers and all the sound bites get transcribed into the computer system, so that writers can look through them and figure out what they want to use for their shows. The tape loggers assign to a given tape a number and transcribe all the relevant information on a template, including where the tape came from, how many seconds or minutes it runs, whether there's a voiceover or natural sound. They give the tape a name, like "Wide Shot, Waco Cult Compound," then put it on a shelf so that when the writers and producers need to put words over a picture of the Waco cult compound, they can do a search in the computer to find it, then come to the counter where the tape loggers work and check out the tape.

The other part of the tape logger's job is to sit in the nearby newsroom where a group of monitors are set up, and when live video feeds come in, to transcribe them directly into the computer, a procedure called raw logging. Let's say a press conference comes in that will need to be turned into a story quickly; the tape logger is there to describe what's coming in or transcribe what the person giving the press conference says. Those who are hired for this job are not experienced typists, so they sometimes miss a few key words, which makes for a very tense and messy situation.

I was promoted to tape logger after working as a script ripper at a little over seven dollars an hour for about seven months. With the promotion came a modest raise: It was a low wage, but it's apparently a matter of supply and demand. If you talk to anyone at a small station, you'll find that he or she works long hours for low pay because there are so many people wanting to break into television.

You can only shine so much as a tape logger. Around CNN, it's widely considered to be the most dismal spot on the track. You work mostly in a small area to the side of the newsroom, and you tend to get blamed for a lot of things that are out of your control. For instance, the tapes from the short-term library—known as "circulation"—are going out, they're coming in, they're being used for shows, they're all over the place, and a lot of times somebody will blow in, in a hurry, and grab a tape without checking it out. When somebody else comes and needs that tape, and it can't be found, the poor hapless logger who is then tending to circulation gets all the guff.

Tape logging is considered worse than script ripping because people tend to stay there longer. You can remain in this job for eight, nine, ten months, and you can imagine how bad it can be spending half your shift looking at a TV screen and transcribing what you see, or in circulation, dealing with people looking for tapes that sometimes can't be found. More than a few people drop out at this stage. That's why a lot of people say that if you can make it through this, you've not necessarily got it made, but at least you've got the staying power that you need in this business.

CNN encourages a certain kind of personal initiative, even if it doesn't exactly reward it. You're encouraged to observe other jobs, to see if you might want to wind up working at a particular post. Hiring is often done from within the existing ranks, since those are the people who know best how CNN operates. Spending a day at the satellite desk, or with a field crew, or beside a writer can be arranged, as long as it's done on your own time. Such an experience also gives you a deeper understanding of how the network runs. This works wonders with some neophytes, who suddenly decide, say, the assignment desk is *it*; the more cynical may find all jobs equally tedious and want nothing to do with any of them.

Many of those in the VJ program are working on their first job after college or graduate school; they have journalism degrees or communication or telecommunication degrees. Some may have ideas about getting themselves on the air, which is very difficult at CNN. But a lot of people who come to the network are not really sure what they want to do; they know they want to be involved in television, yet they don't know whether they want to report, produce in the studio, or produce in the field. When I arrived at CNN, I was pretty sure I wanted be a line producer: the person who puts together the show rundowns (a detailed schedule for all the elements of a show—packaged news stories, commercial breaks, and so on) and is responsible for the overall look of the show.

I was a tape logger about seven months. Then I became a floating production assistant, or PA, and worked directly with two or three newscasts a day. A floating production assistant covers other people's shifts when they are on vacation or they're sick. In that job, you get bounced around from shift to shift and you can't really plan your life more than three weeks in advance. You've got to know all the different shows. You're actually helping out the associate producer, who oversees all the tape for every story on each show. If there are news quizzes, which CNN runs before and after commercial breaks, the PA takes care of that. The PA will copyedit the font information for the news packages and news quizzes—that is, the supers, or the script that appears on the screen identifying interviewees or places—although the fonts are also double-checked by the copy editor to avoid errors. It's a job that's much more involved than tape logger: you're dealing with specific shows; you're talking to producers and writers; you really feel as if you're more involved in the network news process. That job is the reward for suffering through the menial positions. When you are a logger or a script ripper/VJ, while you're working on the news, you're not working with any one show or staff, and you wonder, "What's my contribution, what's my role?" You're not part of a team. And of course, one of the biggest hurdles is the low pay, but they've raised the salaries of the VJs since I was one.

What kept me going was the promise of a payoff in the end, and I could see I was making progress, however slowly. Just being part of CNN was a big boost, although I was always very vague when talking to people about what I did. I would just say something like, "Well, I help put out the newscast." People were always impressed with *where* I worked, but when I got into the specifics of it, their attitude would change to "Oh, I see," and I never knew if this meant "I understand" or "Oh, you poor thing."

CNN really made a name for itself when the Persian Gulf War hit. Everybody worked a lot of overtime, and that energized people to stay there. Historically, at CNN there's been a lot of job mobility because people would stay for a few years and move on. Now CNN has a lot of prestige, so fewer people are leaving, and it's harder to move up the ladder than it was when I started.

TV is tremendously exciting and fun and a real rush. All the deadlines and the adrenaline pumping—I don't know how many professions are like that. I don't think too many are.

Kevin Vineys is a producer for weekend discussion shows at Cable News Network. He has a bachelor's degree in English from the University of California at Berkeley and a master's in communications from the University of Michigan.

2

The Case of the Creepy Mentor

 JASON WALKER

I got into television in a very roundabout way, almost by accident. When I finished college in 1988, I had no idea what I wanted to do, so I moved to New York to stay with a friend, and worked as a model, a waiter, and then as a computer salesman. The salesman job was so awful that one day I just decided I was not going to go into work. Instead, I spent the day walking around Soho. I went into a computer store, and there was a notice on a bulletin board that said, "Writer wanted for upstart computer newsletter." I'd always liked writing, so I decided to go for it.

I got the job, and it paid about $12,000 a year with no benefits. But it was great, because I worked with just one other person, and this was much more interesting than the job I'd left. I was there for about a year, when I saw an ad in the paper for a position at a cable TV guide magazine. I went in for an interview, and I got the job. I started as editorial assistant and worked my way up to associate editor. Not long afterward, the publication laid off half the staff, and I decided I better get my résumé out. I had been writing a column called "Wired," which was very similar to *TV*

Guide's "Grapevine," and interviewing television celebrities. Because I had to set up all these interviews myself, I was dealing with a number of publicists. There were a lot of talk shows in the city, and I decided that the next logical thing to do was to try to land a job in television.

I sent out my résumé, and a woman from the "Sally Jessy Raphael" show called back and left a message, saying, "I got your résumé and it looks good; give me a call." I called back the next day, very nervous and very excited, but she was busy. I kept calling, and she wouldn't return my calls. Someone at the magazine suggested that I set up a correspondence with her. So every time I wrote an interesting article, I sent her a copy of it with a letter letting her know I was still interested in talking to her about a possible job. One day, I noticed an article in *Hollywood Reporter*, which I had to read for my job, saying that this contact had left the "Sally" show and had been made the executive producer of the "Maury Povich Show." An alarm went off in my head: "Ding ding ding—she's hiring!" I immediately sent my résumé and a cover letter by messenger. I always put a lot of effort into the cover letter. I think it's the key to making a connection with someone; it lets the recipient know that you're a nice person, as well as confident and intelligent. In this case, it worked. The new executive producer called me right up.

I interviewed with her and the supervising producer. They asked me what I did at my job, and I showed them a portfolio of my articles. They asked me questions like, "If we were trying to get, say, Delta Burke on the show, how would you get her?" The executive producer told me she thought I would be good as a talent booker or talent coordinator. She liked me, and I went away feeling very confident that I would get a job on the show. After three weeks, I was finally called in for an interview with Maury Povich. He just wanted to see what kind of a personality I had, what I was interested in, what type of work I had done. He just wanted to know that he liked me. He told me this job would be in Los Angeles, not in New York; would I be willing to relocate? Of course, I said, "Yeah, no problem."

The executive producer booked me on a flight to L.A. to meet with a talent executive for the show. She described him as a very powerful executive who had only recently been hired. Interviewing for the job of his assistant, I met with this executive for two days. He had an odd charm about him: He was very funny, very personable, and he cracked dirty jokes. However, he kept stressing to me that he wanted somebody who was going to be loyal. He said, "If you work for me, you're probably going to get other job offers, but I want to know that you're going to be loyal to me." I went away from that interview confident that I could do this job, but I thought that he was a little weird and he gave me the creeps with all his talk about loyalty. After the interview, I went out for a walk, and when I came back to my hotel room I had a message saying the job was mine if I wanted it. I took it—even though I felt my new boss was a little creepy. I called my parents and moved out to L.A. two weeks later.

But even before I got there, my new boss (let's call him "Mr. Boss") kept calling me during my last two weeks at my old job. He wanted to be my mentor and help me at every step. He called once and reached my roommate, and told him, "Don't you worry, we're going to take good care of Jason." Another time he called at work and asked, "Where does your loyalty lie?" I thought, "What the hell is he asking me this for?" But I said, "With the show, of course." He said, "No. Where does your loyalty lie?" I said, "Well, um, with you and the producer in New York." Then he said, "No, with whom does your loyalty lie?" I finally got it. "With *you*." He said, "Right, your loyalty is with me." I knew then I was in for trouble.

We were supposed to book big-name stars for Maury's show, while the producing staff in New York, where the show was taped, booked "real people." When my first day of work rolled around, Mr. Boss told me, "I'm not happy with our office situation, so we're not going in to work. Wait till you hear from me." We were in temporary offices, and he thought they weren't nice enough, and that they didn't have the right equipment or furniture. So he was complaining to the executive at Paramount, which produces "Maury," and we didn't go in to the office until about three o'clock that first day. He started making all kinds of phone calls to complain some more, and I could see from his end of the conversations that he rubbed people the wrong way and that he wasn't going to last on the job. None of these executives were returning his calls.

During that month—it was August—the executive and supervising producers called us every day and asked who we had booked for the show. They were saying, "We want an 'A' name for the first week." In other words, they were saying, "We want a Schwarzenegger; we want a Tom Cruise; we want a Dolly Parton." I was very naive and didn't yet understand what was going on, but apparently agents were afraid that Maury's show would be too much like "A Current Affair," his previous show, which was a tabloid, and wouldn't risk putting their talent on it. Mr. Boss was very calm, calling all these people at the big agencies like William Morris, and it was becoming clear that we were not going to get the "A" names. Mr. Boss came in to the office day after day at about one in the afternoon after calling me all morning on his car phone, telling me he was hard at work, but I was skeptical.

We finally moved into our permanent office, and once again, he didn't like the accommodations. We had typewriters; Mr. Boss wanted computers. We didn't have the right furniture; he didn't like the paint. His relations with the New York staff were becoming seriously strained. He was unsuccessful in signing up any top stars.

The tension grew during September until the relations between the L.A. and New York staffs were very hostile. They would have shouting matches on the phone. My boss would send documents to Maury to show what was going on, saying, "These are the problems I'm having with these people in New York, and they're being too demanding." The woman who had hired me started calling me to get my view on what was going on, and Mr. Boss by this time was sweating bullets. You could just see the pressure building. One day he got into a huge argument with the New York office over the phone, and I went into his office and he told me to pick up line one. I didn't want to listen in, but he insisted, so I picked up the phone, and I was also sweating bullets. The executive producer told him, "If you don't have an 'A' name by Monday, the management wants to terminate your contract. You gotta call in every favor, because this is bullshit!" He said to her, "I don't like your tone; you have no right to talk to me this way!" She said, "I don't care. If you don't have a name by Monday, that's it. I'm sorry."

Nevertheless, he still came in as late as one in the afternoon. He was also submitting expense reports for $500 to $600 a week, including $250 in car phone bills, with the rest in lunches. To me, he was saying, "Jason, don't worry; I'm going to take care of you. I'll go somewhere else, and I'll take you with me." I was terrified I was going to lose my job only two months after I had started, and I didn't want to go with him if he was fired. When the New York staff asked me what was going on and where was Mr. Boss, I didn't want to say anything, because I was caught in the middle. Now *they* started asking me, "Where does your loyalty lie?" This time, I said, "Of course, with the show!"

All this time, my duties were unclear. I was to assist Mr. Boss, but since I saw him so little, there wasn't much for me to do. I did everything from clerical work to calling agents, and I spent a lot of time doing nothing.

I really saw the light when Mr. Boss took his wife and his agent out to an expensive restaurant for their twentieth wedding anniversary, and the meal showed up on his expense report. I realized he wasn't honest, despite his constant admonitions to me that honesty was essential and that "you always have your reputation." Another time he went to the funeral of Frank Capra and was gone all day and called it work time. He had me get him copies of that night's network news tape to see himself in the story about the funeral, and it cost $150. I sent the bill to the New York office on Mr. Boss's instructions, and a staff member called back asking what it was for. Mr. Boss asked me why I had submitted the bill, and denied ever having told me to do so. I'd never been caught in the middle like this. Finally, one of the New York producers called and said, "Jason, we're terminating your boss, but you have nothing to worry about. We're really happy with you." He came in the next day and had it out with me, saying, "I don't know what you're doing behind my back, but I just want to tell you, don't mess with me. I'll get you." He hasn't yet.

Mr. Boss was fired, and I was alone for a month, booking celebrities for the "Maury Povich Show." I'd never done this type of work before, and I didn't know what I was doing, but there I was, the booker for Maury Povich, calling publicists and trying to get stars on the show. I ended up booking the cast of "The Young and the Restless" and the cast of "Dear John," a new sitcom that season. The week after that show aired, *Entertainment Weekly* ran an article asking why in the world anyone would book "Dear John," because no one watched that series. I cut the article out and saved it. I found it ironic, because the show turned out to be a hit.

The producers finally hired a former booker for "Good Morning America" to be my boss. We immediately hit it off, and she was very talented, but I knew she was stepping into a difficult situation and I feld bad for her. They started up with her—"We need 'A' names. We need 'A' names"—but nobody wanted to go on the "Maury Povich Show." Our big sales pitch was that this was not going to be a tabloid show, but still no one trusted us. Eventually the show did become a tabloid like "Geraldo" and all the other daytime talk shows, and because of that we couldn't get any stars to go on.

The pressure was always on, but my new boss always pulled something off at the last minute. We did get a few campy bookings, like Debbie Reynolds and Zsa Zsa Gabor. Then we heard that Tom and Roseanne Arnold's favorite lunch was Chinese chicken salad from Jerry's Deli. We called their production office, and I said I was calling from the "Maury Povich Show," that we wanted to send over a surprise, and that we wanted to know when they would be eating lunch. We sent over lunch for the entire staff from Jerry's Deli. We had to be creative, because it was the only way we were going to get people on the show. Tom and Roseanne were impressed and said they might do the show. The next week, I was at the ACE Cable Awards show, and they were there, so I ran up to them as they were leaving, and I told them who I was, and Tom Arnold just snapped at me, "Yeah, we're gonna do the show," and they walked off.

What we didn't know at that point was that our executive producer had booked Roseanne's mom behind our backs. This was at the time when Roseanne broke her story about being abused as a child, and our executive producer planned to surprise Roseanne and Tom with Roseanne's mom. Of course, Roseanne found out about it, and she refused to do the show. We had been so excited because we finally had an "A" name, and then the producer screwed things up by being dishonest with us, and we ended up with a huge fiasco. We never got an "A" name for the show.

The most fun I had on Maury's show was when a 1970s sitcom had a reunion show on TV, and the whole cast got together except for one former star. A photo of this actress was on the cover of the *Star*, the *Enquirer*, and all the other tabloids; she was quoted as saying that this sitcom had ruined her life, that she hated her costars, and that she would never come back for a reunion. Of course, every TV tabloid and talk show wanted her as a guest. She was the hot child-star-gone-bad. Our producers said, "Get her at any expense! Whatever you have to do, do it!" Somehow, my boss and I got her home number, and we began talking to her, and it became apparent that she was slightly loony. We persuaded her to let us come out to her house, about forty-five minutes from Los Angeles, and bring her airplane tickets to New York, where she would appear on the show. Her home was out in the middle of nowhere, and we had to stop at a local store to ask directions. We followed a guy in a pickup to find it, going over train tracks and through two streams to get there. Her house was so rundown it looked as if nobody lived in it. A guy came to the door and said he was the actress's husband, and that he was a big rock star. He looked like the late John Belushi—crazy. Inside, the house was a pigsty: It had a cement floor, and there was food, dirty dishes, beer cans, and trash strewn everywhere.

The actress came in, and the first thing we noticed was that she had a black eye—she said that it was from a motorcycle accident. She was wearing sweats, her hair was a mess; she looked like a homeless woman. She told us to sit down in the bedroom, where there was only a mattress and some cushions on the floor, and towels covering the windows. We told her about the show, and she said she wouldn't agree to appear or sign anything until she talked to her lawyer. We thought, "Oh, no, this is going to take forever. We're going to have to wait in this house." So while we waited for her to reach her lawyer, her husband came in and said he wrote a new song, and we had to hear it. Well, it sounded like the Grateful Dead, and it was so loud we couldn't even talk. The actress and her husband started dancing around on the furniture. My boss and I looked at each other and just burst out laughing. Here was this woman we grew up watching on TV, bouncing off the furniture.

All this time, the phone was ringing off the hook—Geraldo, "Hard Copy," the *Star*, everyone wanted her, but she was not signing anything until her lawyer called. She and her husband were now singing and dancing and drinking. We knew this was going to be the day from hell, so we told them we were going to get some lunch, because we wanted to take a break. They insisted on coming along. They got in the car, reached over and turned up the radio full volume, and they were hollering and screaming out the windows. We got to the restaurant, and they ordered round after round of margaritas, and when we passed the rack of tabloids on the way out, with her picture on the covers, her husband shouted, "That's my wife!"

Finally we got back to their house, and the actress reached her lawyer, and she signed to go on the "Maury Povich Show." We had to go back the next day to take the couple to the airport, with them screaming out the windows again. But they did the show, and everybody watched it, and it was a huge hit. She was in tears during her interview, telling about how her father had just died and how the sitcom had ruined her life. Maury called the next day and said, "That was the weirdest interview I have ever done in my life," but it didn't matter because it got good ratings.

・ ・ ・

By the next season, everyone I had been hired to work with was fired. Vicki Lawrence's talk show had just started up, and a staff member called me up and hired me as associate producer. Now I come up with show ideas, book real-life people, and write scripts.

This whole experience has really dispelled the legend of Hollywood for me. I'm not impressed with celebrities anymore, because I see and hear the lies that publicists make up about the stars. Everything is exaggerated, and everyone is an egomaniac. I think a talk show is probably the craziest place you could work: The people are just insane. They're always stretching the boundaries of what's normal. They're fiercely competitive, so you're always under stress, and people don't like each other and no one gets along. But it's still fun and exciting. Even a creepy mentor could not chase me out of the business.

> *Jason Walker attended the University of Delaware and majored in international relations. He was associate producer for the talk show "Vicki!" produced by Group W Productions at NBC studios in Hollywood until 1994 and is now a producer for the talk show "Leeza," produced by Paramount Studios.*

3
Finessing the Art of Chyron

CINDY NELSON

When I was in fifth grade, we had to write stories about what we wanted to be when we grew up. I thought to myself, "What's a job that very few people do?" I decided on TV, because you see only four people when you watch TV news. So I've pursued this career ever since fifth grade. I was editor of my high school paper, and I wrote for the student newspaper at Southern Illinois University at Carbondale. I interned as a reporter for a radio station in Anna, Illinois, and did more reporting and anchoring on a news show at a small campus radio station. This was a ten-minute show, which is incredibly long for radio, so the staff had to fill it with anything and everything—even obituaries. I also worked on the station's radio news service, which put out reports on special topics; fortunately, all the experts we needed were right there, because it was a college campus. My colleagues and I put out press releases about the reports on a radio hotline, and radio stations from the area could call and use them.

While still in college, I also worked for a TV station on campus, as did many of my classmates. We had to audition for those jobs, even though we worked for free. The station had daily newscasts, but only one editing bay (the booth with all the editing equipment), so if we needed to finish our stories, we had to wait our turn to edit them. As a result, we were always there—sometimes all night. It was a lot of hands-on work, but of course, it was much slower than real-world TV work.

Before I graduated, I sent out a lot of résumés and résumé tapes, but in retrospect I think it works better when you target a place where you want to work and actually go there and pound the pavement. I think people remember you better when you're in their face and you actually meet them. I had a sister who lived in Columbus, Georgia, and I went down there knowing I wanted to find a job in TV. At that time, Columbus was the 115th-largest television market, and of course it's easier, as someone who's just graduated, to get a job at a smaller market like that one. Smaller markets don't have a lot of money so they hire college kids and don't have to pay them much.

Even so, it was still hard to get a job there. I talked to every TV and radio station in town. Finally after three months I got my first break: a part-time job as a deejay at a radio station. But since I needed a full-time job and wanted to work as a reporter, I continued my job search. When no jobs seemed to be opening up in television, I applied for a job at a bank and eventually was offered a position there. My parents wanted me to take that banking job. But I wanted to use the TV training I had gotten in college.

I'm glad I didn't take the bank job, because I finally got lucky and got a job at WRBL-TV, the CBS affiliate, but I had to be creative to get it. I had been trying to meet with the news director, and I had been calling and calling but could never get an interview. Then a friend of mine came to town and said, "I've got an interview at WRBL." I said, "You're kidding! I can't get in to see this man for the life of me!" So I called the news director back and said, "I'm only going to be in town for a few days, and I want to meet you." He didn't remember who I was—and, of course, I was already living there. He said, "Okay," and that's how I got that job. He asked me the standard questions in my interview, such as: What can you do? Where do you expect to be five years from now?

I was hired to be a part-time chyron operator. Chyron is the name of the equipment that puts the names of people on the TV screen while you see their faces during a news story. The chyron operator types the names into the chyron machine and picks out the typestyles, or fonts—some stations call that person the "fonter." That wasn't what I wanted to do either, but I wanted to get my foot in the door to the newsroom, so I took the job. I was now working part-time at the radio station and part-time at the television station; eventually the TV job became full-time, and I quit the radio station. The TV job was more technical than I had wanted, but I learned all I could while I was there. I was trained to run the cameras and audio equipment and to do other jobs because the station didn't have a large staff and everybody had to pitch in when someone was out. It was a great experience because I got to learn so much.

I had two weeks at most to learn how to operate the chyron machine. Sometimes the names came in late, because reporters—especially sports reporters—were late in returning from their assignments in the field. They gave me their names late, then I had to type them in in a hurry. Some of this work I could do beforehand, during what's called preproduction. But often it was done during the newscast. My first night on the job was a nightmare. I hadn't quite mastered the trick of typing while the newscast was going on, so during the newscast the director asked me for different names, and I had to answer, "I don't have that one yet." That became my standard line that night. He'd ask me for name after name, and I said, "I don't have that one." The director, who was temperamental, finally yelled, "WHAT DO YOU HAVE?!" It was a difficult night, but later he apologized. After that night, every so often I would get the wrong names on the wrong people, but because I knew how to type I quickly learned how to finesse the art of chyron.

Everything I was taught, I picked up quickly. So instead of hiring from the outside, my boss decided to train me to be a director. After six months of chyron, I was promoted. In some markets, you have a news director and a technical editor, but in Columbus the director did both jobs. I directed the nightly newscasts, which was a wild and very interesting experience because I had never been trained to do anything like it. But I wasn't using the skills I wanted to use. I wanted to write, and at the time I still thought I wanted to be a reporter.

As director, I was in charge of the whole crew for the newscast. I told the audio person and the chyron operator what to do, told the tape operator when to start and stop the videotapes of each story during the newscasts. I directed the camera operators and the teleprompter, so at different times during the newscast I would tell the camera person how to set up the shot—that we needed a medium-distance shot of this anchor on this camera or a close-up on that anchor on the other camera. All during this time, the show was going on, and I had to think quickly. I had to set up the next story while the on-camera people were reading the last story, and tell the chyron operator which names I needed, and the tape operator which machine the tape was to go into.

The job was okay, but it was hard, because things were constantly going on, with no breaks, not even during the commercial breaks. During the commercials, I had to make sure the tape operators in the other control room queued up the right commercial (in other words, got the videotape at the beginning of the commercial ready to roll) and rolled it at the right time. In some newsrooms, the other control room is the master control room and its staff takes care of rolling commercials, but in Columbus I had to keep track and let people on the set know how much time was left in the commercials. It was a constant challenge.

The funniest night I remember: We were doing the weather, and we didn't have the best equipment for weather because it was a bare-bones operation. We had videotape with several different maps on it, and we would roll it from our control room. The guy in the master control room was supposed to freeze the videotape on each weather map in turn, so that it showed up on a screen behind the weather forecaster. But this guy was new and I was new, so when we rolled the tape—on which each map came up very quickly—and I asked him to freeze on the first map, he missed it. He missed the next map, and then the next one, till maps were flying by behind the weather forecaster, and he just gave up and didn't freeze on any of them. The tape finally went to black behind her, and she ad-libbed, "It's a dark night in the valley." I panicked and looked for something to put up behind her; finally I just put the radar image behind her and kept my fingers crossed.

While I was in Columbus, I was learning all these skills that would help get me other places, and I knew exactly where I wanted to go. I wanted to get into the editorial side and out of the technical side of the news, and it was obvious to me that it wasn't going to happen in Columbus. I called stations near my home in Cape Girardeau, Missouri, once a month or every other month. I wanted to work for the number-one station in that market, so I called the news director there and told him, over and over, "I want to work for your station." He had met me while I was in college, and knew I was from the area. He also knew I was persistent. Finally the station created a position for me: I was hired as associate producer for the morning news show. (The key to being successful in television is to be persistent!)

My directing experience really helped in Cape Girardeau at the times when my director didn't want to do something that I wanted to do. When he said, "We can't do that," I could say, "Yes, we can." Most of the time he was agreeable, but if it was a day when he didn't feel like doing something, I could tell him we *could* do it, because I knew what was technically possible, and I knew what the shot should look like, that kind of thing.

I was in Cape Girardeau for two years and left there as producer of the morning show. I took a job at a TV station in Nashville, then became a writer for "CNN Headline News," then got a job as a producer for CBS News "Up to the Minute."

I spent a lot of time in Columbus doing what I didn't want to do, which I think is very common in television. But the skills I learned during my first year in TV, including copywriting and editing tapes, have all come in handy. At "Up to the Minute," which is the CBS overnight news show, we try to do everything as economically as possible. I produce two segments, "Newsmap" and "Going Global." Not only am I producing, but I write the copy and edit the videotape to go with the copy. Since the show is trying to save money, I'm a more valuable employee with a variety of skills.

I still have days when I'm not sure I want to stay in this business, but I think I would like to stay, as long as I continue to be challenged and find jobs that I really like. I like my current position a lot. My first job, on the other hand, was disappointing because it was only part-time and the pay was so low. (I *should* have known what I was in for. My college professors had said over and over, "You're not going to make any money in television. But you're doing it because you love it. As a journalist, you have a mission, and this is how you help society. You can't do it for the money." That's very true.)

There are days when I think I am helping, when I feel that I've done some good. I recently booked a lawyer for Haitian refugees at Guantánamo Bay, and another guy who is for immigration reform. I think the plight of the Haitian refugees is important, and our show was giving both points of view and lots of good information. That's when I feel I'm contributing: when I'm actually explaining why things are the way they are, when people are learning something or hearing something that they never heard before.

Cindy Nelson is a producer for CBS News "Up to the Minute." She graduated from Southern Illinois University in Carbondale, where she majored in radio and television broadcasting.

4
The Value of a Long List of Names

MIA FREUND WALKER

At Princeton University, I majored in English, was involved in the school radio station, and had worked on a public affairs radio show. I might have had journalism in the back of my mind, but as an undergraduate, I never consciously decided to pursue a career in television.

After I graduated, I went to work for the Michael Dukakis campaign leading up to the presidential election of 1988. I moved directly out to Iowa for the primaries, and after the Iowa caucuses, I traveled all around the country, working as a congressional district field organizer. While I was working in the general election in Austin, Texas, I got to know a local political reporter who was engaged to my volunteer coordinator. The campaign was big news, and just about everything we did was reported on. I liked this reporter, but I would get so frustrated when issues that I knew firsthand were misrepresented in the press or TV news. It was a weird, larger-than-life experience to be working on a presidential campaign; you read about your job every day, and Mike Dukakis got so abused by the press. I felt that when the campaign was over,

I wanted to be on the other end. Rather than being the person who was the subject of the report, I wanted to be the person reporting—and do a better job of it than the people I had contact with. That was my own small, idealistic ambition; I would change the way the news was reported.

I worked on the Dukakis campaign until November of 1988. After the election, I moved to Boston and began networking wildly. I was interested in getting a job in television news. I must have set up about twenty-five informational interviews in the span of two months. While I was interviewing I was also working for a caterer and for a temp agency, which placed me in a secretarial spot at WBZ, a network affiliate in Boston. (When you're applying for jobs, it's good to be employed, even if you're not employed in the industry. If you're not working at all, people tend to write you off.)

I started interviewing with all the local network affiliates. One night I was invited to watch the eleven o'clock news being produced at the ABC affiliate in Boston. Although I found it very exciting, I wasn't sure it was the route I wanted to pursue. I just wanted to be at a place where people treated each other with respect and believed in what they were doing. Still, I went ahead and met the news director. I was interviewing with anyone who would agree to meet with me, to see what was available. I didn't know the industry, and I wanted to meet people who did.

I ended up interviewing with a producer at WGBH, the Boston PBS affiliate. She didn't have a job for me, but she was a friend of a friend of a friend, so she said she'd at least meet with me. She was enthusiastic, very nice, and we clicked. She gave me the names of a few other producers at WGBH. One of them was a hippy-type, freelance producer, and within a few months of calling him up almost every day (I was just such a pest, but he liked me), he gave me a job as a location scout.

WGBH doesn't have a lot of staff producers; but it does have a lot of freelance producers whose offices are in the same building, and there's enough freelance work that they're there full-time. The production he hired me to work on was an industrial video about business ethics for employees of a major corporation.

As a location scout, I went around to different restaurants to find one where we could shoot a business meeting. It was really fun. This film depicted a client-employee relationship that was awkward and illustrative of ethical issues—the client was making moves on the employee or the employee was being bribed, I can't remember which—and the question was how to deal with it. One of the first scenes had to be in the restaurant to set up the whole context. After I found the restaurant, I had to find an office space where we could shoot a scene showing the employee being put into a difficult situation with the client during a meeting.

Finding the office was easy, too, though it happened through elaborate, Byzantine connections. One of my friends had a friend who was a financial consultant, a kind of venture capitalist. Two of her clients were former employees of the NBC affiliate in Boston. One of them had been the affiliate's business and economics correspondent, and they were starting up their own financial consulting company producing corporate videos. The woman who was a friend of a friend thought I might be interested in talking to them about their experiences at the NBC affiliate. When I had first met with them in their office, they indicated they were interested in me, saying, "This is what we thought of working for the affiliate, but you might want to consider working for us." I had recently met with these people when I was hired as location scout, and now I was interested in their office. They had a great conference room, and I thought, "Aha! If I ask to use their office, they'll know that I'm out there working and it will make them more inclined to hire me once my work at WGBH is finished." I still wanted to make a good impression. So they let WGBH shoot in their office.

By the end of the business ethics project I had done everything from location scouting, buying lunch for the crew, and photocopying to more substantial things like working with talent on continuity supervision (making sure each set looks the same as it did in the last shot).

My WGBH contact had also put me in touch with another WGBH producer, who was going to do a series for PBS. It was to be similar to "Entertainment Tonight," but because this was a public TV station and not a network, the show could *really* be critical of television. My job was to do about four weeks of research. I had to talk to all kinds of television experts and find out what they thought was important to address in a show about television. I had to talk to everyone from intellectuals to technical types; to interview them about how television had become the most powerful cultural medium and how television was supposed to educate. This producer wanted to get all these types together into a seminar, which I think ultimately did happen before he did his pilot. I left long before the pilot was made, but I put together two huge notebooks for him, with conversations with everyone from Fred Friendly, longtime head of CBS News, to professors at the University of Southern California (which has a great training program in television) to Ed Diamond, a television writer for a major magazine. This was a great experience: I got to work out of my home and talk to all these interesting people about television, and then put all the information together. It was like writing a big research paper, and I was up the whole night before it was due. I guess you'd call me a researcher, but I was officially called a freelance researcher/production assistant. Although titles are important, they can mean so many different things in different organizations.

After working on the corporate consulting videos for about six months, I decided I didn't want to be in Boston anymore. I got lists of television people in New York, names from friends of my parents, and from anyone I happened to talk to in Boston. So before I arrived in New York, I had a long list of people to talk to.

One name I had was of a very well-known and respected video editor. She'd been news editor for ABC and NBC in New York and had gone on her own as a freelancer. She was always hired by good production houses to do editing for documentaries, so she knew everybody. I called her up, and she said, "WHO ARE YOU? Why are you calling me?" Very abrupt. I refused to get intimidated, and I said, "Well, you don't know me, but blah blah blah blah . . ." She said, "I'm editing for this company right now, but why don't you call me back whenever, and here's my home number, but call me at work." She hadn't been very nice the first time, but the second time I called she was so nice, it was like night and day. (A word of advice: Don't get intimidated by people who aren't nice on the phone at first. Keep trying; you never know.) She cheerfully began the conversation, "Oh, hi, I was just thinking about you!" She acted as if we'd grown up together. Then she said, "You know, the company that I'm editing for right now is doing a documentary about Israel. Their associate producer just left, and I think their production assistant is moving up. They've been interviewing all week for a new PA, so you should come to my office and meet me and I'll tell you about the job."

Before meeting with this editor, I went to an interview at Nickelodeon, which went pretty well. Later that day, I went to the postproduction facility of the company where the editor was working. She told me that this was an independent production company specializing in documentaries, pieces that had a lot of integrity. The documentary she mentioned was for PBS, about the

Israelis' reaction to the Intifada. Being Jewish and very interested in Israel, I thought I'd be totally engrossed in this; it would be a great experience. The company had done a lot of other highbrow things, and compared to working for a big place like Nickelodeon, this job would give me a lot more exposure to the different aspects of production. After a while, the editor said, "It's silly for you to talk just to me, because I couldn't hire you: I'm just a freelance editor. So why don't I call the current PA, and she'll come down and interview you."

I had a very good meeting with the PA, who was about a year younger than me. (Be prepared to have a boss who is younger than you, especially if you are starting your career in television a couple of years after college. Age does not always equal experience.) She asked me to come back the next day and meet with the producer, who was the head of the company.

The next day I met the producer—and everybody else in the company. I really liked them all. They seemed completely down to earth. The company had a much more genuine feel to it than some of the other places that I'd been. People didn't have an attitude; they were completely straightforward.

This was on a Wednesday, and I was planning to take that entire week to look around, not start a job until September, a month away, and take a much-anticipated vacation in between. The president of the company said he'd have an answer for me that afternoon. He called back that day with an offer.

I was thrilled, but I tried to temper my enthusiasm because the beginning salary was pathetic. I said, "I want you to know this is a cut from what I was making in Boston, and the cost of living in New York is higher, and I want some sort of assurance that I'll get a raise in the relatively near future. I won't be able to live on this very long, but I'll show you I can work hard. I also want a sense that I'll have some chance to move up." He said, "Absolutely, the company's growing. We'd like you to start tomorrow." So much for my vacation.

Despite the modest salary, I felt very lucky, because I knew that many people had been interested in this job and it was just a fluke that I had managed to get an audience during the first week of interviews. My new boss, who was the president of the company, had been at ABC News for about fifteen years, and had done very well and won Emmys for his segments there, and had won a lot of credibility with his own company as well. During his company's first year or two in operation he had won an Emmy for an HBO documentary on John Kennedy. I was lucky to hop on board when the company was still fairly young, only about three years old.

I arrived at work the next morning, filled with excitement. I was handed a one-hundred-page script and taken down to the copy machine (which didn't collate) at the postproduction facility and spent the next four hours copying, one page at a time. Welcome to television!

During my first year I ran a lot of errands, bought supplies, answered the phone, did photocopying. I was in on a lot of the meetings as the staff was developing the script for the Israel documentary. I soon became very good at fact checking. I remember calling my rabbi a lot to help me check facts. (That's another key for people going into this business: Don't be shy about using your resources right away. Don't be afraid to call anyone you might know who might know anything about the issues. You should just assume that's part of your job.)

Later I got more involved with setting up interviews, doing research over the phone, learning about archival footage houses where we got archival footage for many of the documentaries we did. We did another documentary on Bobby Kennedy, and another one on the New York Public Library for PBS. Once I became more involved, I really loved doing research and production.

The production assistant who initially met with me left after about a year, and I was thrilled that her job wasn't filled for almost another year, because it meant more responsibility for me. I got to go out in the field more, for example, on an ABC special with Barbara Walters on genetic engineering. I got to spend weeks at a time at a hospital setting up interviews and getting the women who were about to have babies lined up to go on camera.

By the time I left, I was working as an associate producer on a series we were doing, updating old "20/20" segments. It was a joint venture with Discovery and ABC News. I was very involved in finding the characters from interesting old segments and interviewing them, filling in the details of the intervening years.

I think that company was a great place to cut my teeth. My job started out as a menial position, but I managed to spend three and a half years there, and left as associate producer to become a freelance associate producer on a "Frontline" documentary.

Mia Freund Walker is currently the story editor at ABC's "20/20." Her background includes the production of corporate videos as well as public and network television.

5
Cosell Wore Sunglasses

PETER MEHLMAN

I started my career in 1980 as a copy aide for the *Washington Post*. The paper offered me the job sight unseen, but there was just one problem: Because somebody had told me the *Post* wasn't hiring white males, I had written my letter to the *Post* as a woman. I ended up writing another letter explaining why I had misrepresented myself. Fortunately, I was hired anyway and worked as a copy aide a little more than two years. The job was mostly answering phones and running errands, but I also wrote a lot of sports stories and anything else I could get.

I wanted to move to New York, but it didn't seem likely that I'd get a job at the *New York Times* so I thought I'd try TV. I was interested in the show "SportsBeat" with Howard Cosell, and I submitted a fairly amusing letter. (I don't recommend writing a humorous letter unless you're really sure you can pull it off.) I also had some people from the *Washington Post* who knew Cosell put in a good word for me. The job interview—for the position of production assistant—was with Cosell himself. It was in his office, and I don't remember the light being particularly bright—he had his back to the window—but he wore sunglasses.

Howard Cosell, you must understand, is someone I had idolized for years. I had seen him on TV; I had read all his books. I thought that the interview was going pretty well, when he asked me who I thought was another good sports journalist on television. It was a key moment. I believed that I had inside information, having heard that everybody thought that Brent Musburger from CBS was a really good journalist, even though I'd never seen any evidence of it. I mentioned Brent Musburger, and Cosell started laughing. Suffice it to say, I got the job anyway. He kidded me about that forever. He'd always joke, "Well, you could go work for Brent!" Sometimes he would just walk into my office and casually say, "So, what are your plans?" as if I were going to be let go at any moment, and he'd say, "I'm sure Brent will take you on." He never let me live that down.

"SportsBeat" was very much like "60 Minutes," except it was all sports journalism. The staff was very small, so everybody could have a variety of responsibilities. Sometimes I got to write Howard's scripts. I also did research, graphics, and other technical stuff. It was really good experience. Howard kind of sequestered his employees, keeping them apart from the rest of ABC Sports. What I saw of it was very shallow and superficial. At the *Washington Post*, I had met and worked around people who were tremendously dedicated to journalism, really bright people. But ABC Sports put more of an emphasis on maintaining the image of ABC Sports—this was during its heyday in the early 1980s—than on being good journalists. For example, ABC loved the kind of employee who would drive to the airport, leave the rental car at the curb, and throw the keys through the window as he or she ran out to meet the plane. There was an unbelievable amount of corporate waste at the time. (The network, like so much of corporate America, has tightened its belt in the 1990s.)

Although "SportsBeat" was never a popular show, it was critically acclaimed and won a lot of Emmys. Howard believed that sports and the real world were inextricably connected. He was great at helping you learn how to think, looking at a sporting event and seeing beyond the usual this-guy's-a-great-hitter story. He'd look for things that were interesting or amusing or hypocritical. We did an entire show about the law of eminent domain, because there was a big controversy about the Oakland Raiders moving out of Oakland. The city of Oakland was considering trying to keep the team there under eminent domain. There weren't many sports shows doing a whole show or even a story about eminent domain. We did a story about the future of pay-TV and sports, a half-hour story about how everything that you've gotten used to watching for free, you might eventually have to pay for. The Olympics, the World Series, the Super Bowl—all might become pay-per-view. That was a fascinating piece, and it had everybody screaming things like, "It's un-American to have to pay to watch the Super Bowl on TV." I remember David Stern, who is now the commissioner of the NBA, saying, "No, it's not un-American to have to pay for those things. To have a product that you can sell, and give it away, *that's* un-American." It was the perfect example of how Cosell could get a dialogue going.

I felt very comfortable around Howard. I think that was partly because he was an interesting and fun guy to be around, and partly the folly of youth—I was twenty-four at the time. I remember that one of my first weeks on the job, he said, "I can't wait to get to the Hamptons." I had a share of a house at the Hamptons with about twenty friends, so I said, "Oh, do ya have a half-share out there, Howard?" This to a man with millions! Howard got a kick out of being kidded in this way. If you could make jokes like that, if you could abuse him, he loved it. Once I went to a wedding on a Sunday, and it was black-tie. For some reason, I just thought it would be funny if I wore the tux to work the next day. Howard was completely befuddled. I heard later that he went into another room and asked a staffer, "Eddie, why is the kid wearing a tux?" And for weeks after, I'd come in and he'd say, "Why aren't you wearing your tux? This is a formal office."

Howard was a blast to be around. I just loved the man. He tried to make us work hard, but I resisted. There were a lot of hours, and Friday nights we had postproduction discussions after that day's taping. I liked doing the interviews, and the preinterviews, and writing scripts. Shooting on location was fun—I got to go to a lot of places in the middle of the country that I'd never been to. I got to meet some tremendous people. I'd say the most memorable person I met was Roger Maris of the New York Yankees. He had had a huge home-run streak in 1961, and had been vilified by the media, who at that time were very protective of Babe Ruth's record. Here he was, having the best season of his life, and he was such a shy man, he was traumatized by it. Clumps of his hair were falling out. It was just awful.

Sports is a strange world, and I was increasingly disgusted by it. I saw what Howard called the "jock-ocracy." I'd been a sports fan all my life, but at that point I developed a huge disdain for sports fans and sportswriters. Maybe ten sportswriters in America are worth their salt.

I made plenty of mistakes. One time, we needed a few photographs—we sometimes shot videotape of certain still pictures. After picking them up, I took a taxicab back to the studio and left the pictures in the taxi and lost them. The senior producer yelled at me at the top of his lungs, "Do something like that one more time and you're fired!" I said, lamely, "Well, it's not like I do it all the time."

Despite the lost photos, I got more and more responsibilities as time went on. Eventually I was expected to come up with ideas for segments. Howard would hire people who knew nothing about sports: He just wanted people who could think. By contrast, I once had an interview for a CBS sports reporting job, and the interviewer asked me questions like, "Who led the NFL in rushing last year?" You could see the difference.

I was at "SportsBeat" for three years, from 1982 to 1984. Amazingly enough, I got laid off. After the Olympics of 1984, ABC was cutting back staff in all departments. "SportsBeat" had very little turnover, so out of eleven people, the three or four with the least seniority were let go. Leaving the show was both traumatic and good (good because it was time for me to move on). I knew I would miss the "family" feeling at Cosell's show. When you're around somebody like Cosell—a guy who regularly made both the most-loved and most-hated-in-America lists—it's like being part of a presidential administration. You have a very close-knit, family kind of feeling, which is a real good thing.

After I was laid off, I looked around for jobs and slowly gravitated toward magazine writing. I was thinking about how after you're dumped by your girlfriend, you can't eat for weeks, so I wrote up a whole diet called the "We Just Broke Up Last Night Diet"—I really had a lot of time on my hands—and ended up sending it to *Mademoiselle* magazine, which bought it. I made a living at freelance writing for a while, and it was a lot of fun and gave me a lot of freedom—a very good job for a lazy person. Then I moved to L.A., thinking it would be an interesting place to live. I wasn't moving here for television: I was going to continue writing for magazines. But I got a new word processor when I got out here, and just to try it out, I did a when-in-Rome thing: I wrote a TV script for "The Wonder Years." I figured the process was just like that for magazines: Write the script, send it to the

TV show, and the show buys it. But I was given a rude awakening. I showed the script to my cousin, who was in the TV business, and he thought it was really well done; nevertheless, he said, "The chances of the show buying it are about ninety-nine to one, and that's *good* odds. Your script might get you an agent. That's the best you can really hope for." So I sent it to agents, and got rejected by many of them, and one of them liked it. Then I ran into Larry David, the executive producer of "Seinfeld." I had met him in New York, and we had a lot of mutual friends. He knew that I wrote, and he said, "Why don't you give me some writing samples, and I'll pass them on to Jerry." Several other people I knew had gotten the same offer from Larry, and Jerry had said "thanks but no thanks," so I was fairly apprehensive about doing this, but I gave him my "Wonder Years" and an "About Men" column I'd written for the *New York Times*. The latter was a pretty funny piece about this day I'd spent after I'd broken up with my girlfriend. I wasn't used to going solo in New York, so I spent the day walking around the city trying to spot a celebrity. I think the "About Men" column caught Jerry's fancy. Larry called me back and said, "Jerry said, 'Sign him up.'"

I have now been working on the "Seinfeld" show for four years. Writing a sitcom is very liberating because you don't have to deal with any facts. Whereas I used to worry about people thinking I'm making up my quotes, now I do nothing *but* make up quotes. You don't have to worry about libel. It's been a fabulous experience.

Peter Mehlman graduated from the University of Maryland, where he majored in history and basketball playing. He is now producer for "Seinfeld."

6

People Skills and Passion

DEB MCDERMOTT

Radio was the only news reporting I did in college, at South Dakota State University. I never thought I'd go into television. I worked at the public radio station, which was the college-owned station. I received credit for reporting, very minor stuff. I had studied basic print journalism and had the option of going into advertising or broadcast; I chose advertising and took marketing and graphics courses.

I needed to do an internship—it was required for my degree. I really wanted a PR job when I graduated, so between my junior and senior years I looked for a PR internship. My uncle, who happened to be governor of South Dakota at the time, said that he could get me a job with the state tourism department, but I really didn't want to rely on my uncle. It obviously helps to have contacts, but nepotism wasn't my thing. So I sent out letters, including one to Western Airlines in Los Angeles, which is one of the few airlines that serve South Dakota. Western expressed an interest in me, and after an interview over the telephone I was offered an internship. I thought that was great, but then I found out there was no pay! I called back and said, "I'm really sorry, I want to do this, but I don't have enough money to come out there for the whole summer. I don't have any relatives to stay with or anything." The company eventually offered to pay me $500 a month, and I said, "All right!" I got in my car with a girlfriend of mine and headed for Los Angeles. We lived in Redondo Beach, a block from the ocean, and we had a great time. The experience gave me another look at the world outside of South Dakota. I had never ventured much outside my home state—my entire childhood was spent in the same city, and I went to college in my hometown. I had taken a trip to Europe the summer after my freshman year, but other than that I was a sheltered Dakotan.

I came back, completed my senior year, and graduated in the spring. But before I graduated, I did everything I possibly could so that I had experience to show. I sold advertising for the university's sports program, I organized concerts on campus, raised lots of money with fund-raisers, did public relations for the campus ministries. This was all volunteer, of course; I was never paid for any of it. I loved PR. At the same time, I was working full-time at a grocery store and also working part-time at a clothing store all through college.

In addition, I was a head cheerleader and—this will sound kind of strange—it was a good experience because it taught me to manage people. We had a squad of sixteen, and I practically lived with them from mid-August through April. We had no budget, so we had to raise all of our money to travel and for uniforms. I had to make sure that people got along and were disciplined, that they came to practice every day at 6:30 A.M. (because it was too hard to get everyone together after late classes). I planned the trips. We had an adviser, one of the coaches, who may have helped us with the tryouts, but we pretty much ran it ourselves. It was great experience.

The most important thing for a student looking for jobs is to get as much experience as possible. Today, when somebody comes to me seeking employment, and doesn't have anything to show me on his or her résumé, or maybe has done one internship only because it was required, that person is just not going to get the same opportunity as somebody else who has a lot to show.

I got out of school during a recession, and kids were having a horrible time finding jobs. I interviewed for every PR job you could possibly imagine—anything that came along I'd go interview for. I think the hardest thing for students is finding out exactly *where* the jobs might be. So I was knocking on doors and going places and getting rejected. I spent a lot of time in South Dakota looking because that's where I lived, but I kept hearing things like, "Well, you were a strong candidate but we hired somebody with more experience." I went to Omaha, where one of my brothers lived, and stayed there while I interviewed, and also to Lincoln, Nebraska, where I have another brother, and I interviewed for PR jobs in hospitals and school systems, with AAA and ad agencies—everywhere.

I finally talked to a woman who was the president of the ad club for Omaha. She suggested a couple of agencies and other places I might try, and then she said, "I heard the promotions and public relations director's job is open at KOLN"—which is the CBS affiliate in Lincoln—"but I'm not sure they're going to hire anyone just out of college, because the woman who is leaving has been there for ten years." So I went through all my other leads first. I tried everything else, and I got down to the end of my list and there was nothing—no jobs—and I was so depressed. I remember sitting in my brother's house in Omaha, thinking, "I'm never going to find a job!" But then I thought, "Well, I'll call this station over in Lincoln, and maybe I can get an interview there." I did manage to get an interview, during which I didn't let the interviewer talk at all! I had gone through my spiel so many times before, it was second nature to me now. And I had brought along a lot of things to discuss: advertisements I had designed, radio copy and press releases I'd written, stuff on tape—a complete portfolio of all kinds of material. After going through my whole spiel, the interviewer let me talk to somebody else, and to somebody else again.

The position I was interviewing for was head of the department, which included supervising three people. And I'd never been inside a television station except for an interview! When we got all through, I walked out and said to myself, "I'm never going to get that job! The interview was a good experience, but nothing will come of it." A week later, however, I got a phone call and was asked to come back for another interview. At that interview, I was offered the job.

I literally was so shocked, I blurted out, "Oh! Oh. Oh. Oh!" This was a Thursday, and I actually said, "Well, um, can I get back to you? Can I let you know on Monday whether or not I'm going to take this job?" Now they were shocked! "You're not going to take the job?! . . . Well, there's a problem: We'd really like to have a decision by tomorrow morning because the woman you're replacing is in Chicago right now at a CBS star weekend, and this is something that you're going to be in charge of next year, and it would be good for you to go to Chicago and learn what she does." So I said, "Well, I'll call you by tomorrow morning."

My fear was that I wouldn't be able to do the job, and that's why I didn't accept it on the spot. I thought, "My god! I'm going to start at the top and go down!" I had never thought of working at a television station, and I had no idea that I would be offered this job. I went back to Omaha, and I talked to my high school sweetheart, whom I was still dating and who had gotten a job in

Omaha. This boyfriend, Kevin, who is now my husband, kept saying to me, "I thought we were going to get married! How can you be in Lincoln when I'm in Omaha?" I talked to my father and to each of my four brothers, and they all said, "You're taking the job! Don't let any guy persuade you not to take this job! It's a great job! Take the job!"

So I accepted the job and got on an airplane the next morning. Now, what you have to understand is that I'm from South Dakota, and I had never flown on an airplane by myself before. I had worked for Western Airlines, but not *on* an airplane. I did not know how to buy an airplane ticket. I didn't have a credit card—I didn't have a job, so how could I have a credit card, right? I talked to my dad, who said, "I'll make a reservation for you and put money in your account. All you have to do is buy the ticket." It was just so stupid, not knowing how to do any of this. I got on the airplane, arrived in Chicago at eight in the evening, and though I had the address of the hotel where I'd be staying, I wasn't sure how to get there! I thought I had to take a bus! I didn't know that businesspeople just hopped in a cab. I could never imagine spending all that money on a cab. So I got on a bus, and it took me an hour and a half to get from O'Hare to downtown, stopping at every hotel along the way.

When I finally got to my destination, a big cocktail party was in full swing. It was the kick-off party for star weekend, which was a weekend when all the stars of the upcoming season's shows would come to Chicago, and stations from all over the country would send crews to do interviews that could be used for promotions.

The woman I was replacing and her crew would be shooting for four other stations, so a lot of confidence had been placed in them. They'd be in a hotel suite, and all these stars would come through for interviews. That night at the kick-off party, all the stars were there, and I was thinking, "Oh, my god, what have I done? Here I am, I don't have the foggiest—I don't even know what a camera is—I don't know anything about producing anything! What am I doing here?"

I spent the entire weekend learning what was going on. Every hour a different star or set of stars from a television show would come into our hotel suite to do interviews with the reporters from the four stations we were representing, and my job was to executive-produce the whole thing: to make sure we could accommodate everybody in the suite, make sure the quality shots were there, make sure that everybody was happy. I had never done anything like that before, so the whole thing was new, but I had had experience getting a lot of people together to get something done, so I was able to do it.

The person I was replacing was wonderful and today is one of my close friends. Instead of looking at me like a young punk, a college kid, she was supportive and helpful and continued to be the entire time I worked there. That first night after the cocktail party, I went back to my hotel room, and I called Kevin, and I cried on the phone and said, "I don't think I can do this!" But I did. I went back, and I worked at that station for seven years, and the people who worked for me at first thought "Who is this they hired to be our boss?!" But I learned television and never got fired.

I was responsible for the TV clips promoting the television station, all public relations, press releases, and special projects. The beauty of it was that people were really willing to help me. A photographer in the engineering department was willing to sit down and teach me everything about shooting and editing. It was a small but a well-equipped station, and its ratings were phenomenal. The staff had faith in me in part because the woman I had replaced had also been hired right out of college, and they really liked that. Plus, I was cheap, very cheap.

Although I was smart enough to know that I didn't know anything, I was naive enough to think that I could learn everything. I've always felt lucky that I have this eternal optimism that I can basically do what I want to do. I guess as you grow older you lose a little bit of that, and reality sets in, but especially then, if I believed I could do it, I could convince others I could do it too. As I grew more experienced, I would go to Paul, the station manager who had hired me, and say, "I want to try something else now. Give me some more to do." So he'd give me more to do, and I kept learning.

The biggest mistakes I made had to do with dealing with people. I thought I was pretty good at handling people, but I learned very quickly that there was a big difference between the people I was used to dealing with when I was in college—kids who were the same age as me—and the people who were employees of the station—who often had spouses and children and more complicated personal problems. I was also dealing with people's perceptions of me and my perceptions of them. As I was trying to figure out ways of getting things done, I tended to be too direct, saying, "This is what we should do and this is why we should do it," rather than considering how my idea might affect the people I was working with. They might be a lot more structured than I am, more set in their ways. I was a department head, and the other department heads' average age was about fifty, so when I was talking about making changes, to me it was no big deal, but to them it was changing the way they'd done business for a long time. That's an adjustment that I didn't quite anticipate, learning how to get things done in an organization with lots of different types of people.

As it turned out, the station had made a good decision in hiring me, because I had a lot of skills that you can't learn on the job at a TV station. The station could teach me the ins and outs of its operation, but not how to do press releases and radio advertising and all that—that's something I brought with me.

I did learn some of the technical side of television. I know this dates me, but in 1976 we got our first TK76 camera, which was the first portable video camera. Before then, only film was used in the field. This was the first video-deck camera, and I learned how to operate it with a photographer-engineer at the station. He was young, probably ten years older than I was, and very creative. He had run a film camera before, so he and I would go out and shoot, the come back and edit to music. We could be much more creative with video because it was so much faster and easier to work with than film. It was a whole new art form!

Everybody loved the woman I replaced. She was very good at what she did. She was a difficult act to follow, but she left good records and complete files, and whenever I had a question I'd call her. For example, less than a month after I started the job, the station sponsored a Pro-am golf tournament that she had organized when she was there. I was completely unprepared for this event, but she literally walked me through everything I was supposed to do, and I was able to do it. If she had not been there to support me, I probably would have fallen flat on my face.

Paul, the general manager, became my surrogate father, and after about a year there, I decided that I wanted to be what Paul was—general manager of a station—when I grew up.

I even wrote it down on a piece of paper as a promise to myself. I was twenty-five, and my husband and I asked each other what we wanted to be doing in ten years. "When I'm thirty-five years old, I'm going to be general manager of a television station. I want to be making this much money. I want to take two vacations a year." I had it all laid out, and I tucked the note away somewhere and forgot it. I found it again when I was moving to Nashville. I was moving there as station manager, and I was general manager by 1990. I just chuckled at the way my dream had become a reality.

I ended up working in Lincoln for seven years, getting more and more responsibility, and when I left I had eighty people reporting to me. When I left, Paul said, "Oh, I'm so disappointed you're leaving, because I really wanted you to replace me." That made it hard to go, but I knew I was making the right decision, because I felt I wouldn't be the best at a general manager's job if I never worked anywhere else, if I only worked in one place, and hadn't had the experience of working at different kinds of stations.

I think I knew at a very young age that I wanted to be a general manager because my strength has always been managing people. My philosophy is to adapt my management to the person. Obviously I don't become a hypocrite, changing completely depending on whom I'm dealing with, but I do realize that people are different and I've got to manage them differently. My role is to learn someone's weaknesses, then help them overcome their weaknesses and support their strengths, and let them be independent in the areas in which they're strong.

The luckiest thing that ever happened to me was getting a job in television. My husband often says to me, "You ought to be paying *them*, you're having so much fun! This isn't a real job." I've found that most of the people who work in television have a passion for it; they wouldn't do anything else. I can't imagine doing anything else, not even being bumped up to corporate. I wouldn't want to *not* be at a television station.

Every day is a new surprise, good or bad. My colleagues and I also have an opportunity to make a difference. We can entertain people—make them laugh or make them cry—but we can also help people. Second Harvest Food Bank in Nashville can call us up and say that it's out of baby food, and we can run a story and it'll end up with $15,000 in donations and truckloads of baby food. That makes me feel good. Most general managers I know really wanted this job—there's nothing else they wanted to do—and they love their job. In most cases, you just don't stumble into the job of general manager. The first job you may stumble into—just dumb luck sometimes—but after that, it's a passion, and you get there because you *want* to get there.

Deb McDermott is general manager of WKRN-TV and the first female head of a television station in Nashville. She has served as president of the National Association of Television Program Executives, as a member of the board of governors of the ABC Television Affiliates Association, and has presided over her station's precipitous rise in news ratings.

7
Why Is the Bird Up on the Router Switch?

SARA JUST

When I was about eleven years old I decided I wanted to be a journalist. More than a couple of friends suggested, only half kidding, that journalism might be a practical application for my naturally nosy personality.

While I was earning a bachelor's degree in American history at Columbia University and reporting for the campus daily newspaper, I pursued internships in journalism. Internships, I was advised, enable you to get a glimpse at want it's really like to work in your chosen field. While I knew I was interested in the news, I wondered which medium might suit me best.

The summer after my freshman year I did an internship at the local ABC affiliate in Boston, WCBV. I was assigned to work with consumer affairs reporter Paula Lyons, who patiently let me watch and learn as she reported and produced nightly stories. The next summer I reported for the suburban newspaper in my hometown in Massachusetts. It was the first time I had been published anywhere other than a student newspaper. The next summer, between my junior and senior years in college, I was selected to be an intern at *Time* magazine. There I was able to contribute to the kinds of stories that I most enjoyed reading: breaking national and international news. That year I had also worked as the editor-in-chief of my college's daily newspaper, *The Spectator*. These experiences convinced me that the notion I first held at age eleven would not change. I wanted to be a professional journalist.

In 1988, as my college graduation neared, I applied for jobs in both print and television news—still unclear which medium to pursue. In response to the résumés sent to some forty-five newspapers and twenty-five local TV stations, I received a beautiful collection of rejection letters. I contemplated wallpapering my dorm room with them. Finally, I was called for a few interviews, which eventually turned into three job offers at small and midsized newspapers. I chose to accept an offer from *The Patriot Ledger* of Quincy, Massachusetts, which was the largest and most respected newspaper that offered me a job.

I worked for nearly a year as a "town" reporter. This title meant that I was responsible for covering all the news that occurred in my town—everything from committee hearings of the zoning board and meetings of the school board to features and profiles. I was expected to write at least one story a day, which gave me a lot of valuable writing experience. The editors were extremely helpful and in many ways served as teachers for some of the more inexperienced reporters like me. One editor whose supervision I especially valued was Jason Seiken. Often he would do more than just edit my articles: He would tell me what was wrong with them, send them back to me, and tell me to do it over again. This process was time consuming for him as well as for me, but it taught me how to compose the articles to my own satisfaction rather than simply rely on a good editor to fix them for me.

The news gods smiled on me while I was at the *Ledger*. In addition to the typical stories one covers in a middle-class suburban town, the state sited a sewage landfill in my town, causing a great deal of local protest. As one of my favorite writers, Dave Barry, once said about his days covering suburban news, I learned everything there is to know about sewage. The sewage story continued for months, landing my stories on the front page with regularity.

At the same time, I was not particularly happy the year I was at the *Ledger*. While the paper was a terrific opportunity for me, it also happened to be located in the area where I grew up. After four years at Columbia, I missed New York. Furthermore, the internship and subsequent part-time stringing work I did at *Time* magazine had given me a taste of covering major news stories, and I was a little bored covering local news.

So when a friend who was working at ABC News called to say there was an opening there, I jumped. It was an opportunity to be around national and international news again, as well as move back to New York. Unfortunately, it was also television, and by that point I was becoming something of a print snob. Would I be losing my chance to be a print reporter if I sampled the world of television news?

But I didn't have a lot of time to ponder my choice. Moments after hanging up the phone, someone from the network's personnel office phoned me. My friend must have mentioned my interest immediately. Since I had once interviewed there for an entry-level desk assistant job while I was still in college, they had my résumé and had already checked my references. They offered me a desk assistant position at "Nightline," one of my favorite programs, but said I had to make the decision to accept the job within a few hours and start in two weeks or the opportunity would be lost. I spent the whole morning pacing and calling friends and family for advice.

A lot of people thought I was making a mistake in leaving the newspaper, that I was on the right track, paying my dues, and that it was a better place to learn to write and report. Some argued that going to an entry-level job in television, where I'd primarily be answering phones, filing, and running people's errands, would be a step backward.

I was in quite a quandary. To make matters worse, one of my best friends, whose advice I often relied on, was in the middle of a cross-country driving trip. I called his mother, thinking she might know how to reach him, and I told her about my dilemma. Her response was, "You have no strings on your life now, no responsibilities. Take a risk. You've been responsible in your choices up until now, at college, doing internships, extracurricular activities. If this is something you're curious about, give it a try. What do you have to lose?" What sound, reasonable advice, I thought. I immediately called ABC and accepted their offer.

I told everyone that it would be an experiment. I would give television one year, and if it didn't feel right for me I would go back to newspapers.

At "Nightline" I was answering phones, organizing faxes—all of which somebody had done for *me* at the newspaper. It was something of a shock and required me to swallow a little pride. But I soon learned that a desk assistant is very much like an apprentice. While photocopying scripts, retrieving videotapes from the library, and transcribing interviews, I had an opportunity to watch and understand how a show is put together. I tried to understand what was happening and get involved. If a producer was working on a story about a subject I had recently read about, I might clip the article and mention it. Or if I knew of a professor from Columbia who might make a good interviewee on a program that was coming up, I would make a suggestion. I tried to participate as much as possible, without ignoring office responsibilities.

After I had been at "Nightline" for a little while, and had demonstrated my enthusiasm and competence, several producers gave me opportunities to learn more. Some would take me along as they worked in the field, conducting interviews and shooting "b-roll"—the pictures that help set the scene for a story but are not actually part of the interview. I remember how thrilled I was when a producer asked me to go on a shoot with a camera crew by myself. It was a story on the closing of the long-running Broadway musical "A Chorus Line." The producer had completed the interviews but needed a picture of the dance studio where some of the original dancers in the show first practiced, a simple shot that would last only a couple of seconds, he said. I went with the camera crew downtown to the studio, which had since closed. We shot every possible angle of this building: pan up, pan down, pan left, pan right. I suspect the camera crew knew they were with a novice, but they were patient with me. If you watched the show and blinked you missed the shot, but I was proud of it.

All of these phrases, like "shoots" and "pan right," were a new language when I first arrived at ABC. I needed an instant education in television terminology. At first I was a little nervous. I would answer the phone moments before airtime, and a voice would scream, "The bird is up on router switch twenty-nine!" I would turn to the other, more experienced, desk assistant and repeat the sentence verbatim and ask, "What the heck does that mean?" Before I caught on to the lingo, I sometimes imagined that the words were designed to confuse. But now I realize how helpful it is to have a set of words and phrases that everyone in the workplace understands and recognizes quickly. Often there aren't simple, satisfactory words in ordinary English to explain some of the aspects of television technology.

Even though much of the work I did was menial, I was immediately drawn to the atmosphere and suspected that television was where I belonged. As a newspaper reporter there is a lot of solitary time spent in front of a computer screen writing a story. Producing a television story is largely a group effort. There are so many people involved: the anchors, the producers, the correspondents, the editors, the camera operators. Everyone involved must have the same goals and commitment to excellence. When a program succeeds, all those people can be proud of the product together.

The months that I worked as a desk assistant were an exciting time for a first exposure to television news. Within weeks of my starting at ABC, the 1989 crackdown on the Tiananmen Square uprisings took place. Later that year there was the earthquake in San Francisco and the fall of the Berlin Wall. The news just kept coming. As a former history major, I was thrilled to be there to see it all happen, helping to cover history in the making.

After I had been a desk assistant about six months, there happened to be an opening in the "Nightline" research department. The job intrigued me because it involved reporting and news sense.

I felt comfortable with the demands of this job: gathering information and checking sources. As a researcher I put together background materials, such as articles, statistics, and other information that might assist the producer and correspondent in preparing a story. I was also responsible for checking the facts included in the program's taped report. This required not only accuracy but swiftness. Because "Nightline" is a daily broadcast, correspondents aren't always able to write a script more than a couple of hours before airing. So we researchers had to move quickly.

My new fact-checking responsibilities occasionally gave me nightmares about letting an erroneous piece of information slip through my fingers and onto the air, resulting in humiliation for the program and the network. Luckily nothing like that ever happened. But there were occasional oversights—caught in time, I'm relieved to say—that reminded me always to be cautious and aware.

One example comes to mind. One of my responsibilities as researcher was to write a short briefing packet for the anchor on each nightly subject. On the day that we were doing a story about the expected release of the hostages in Lebanon, I prepared a background packet for Ted Koppel overviewing the years that these men had been held captive. I was trying to provide some specific details that might illustrate all that these men were missing in their lives while in captivity. For instance, some of the hostages had had parents die; others had missed children's graduations, siblings' weddings, and so on. In gathering materials about Terry Anderson, the hostage held longest, I was told that he had a daughter born six years earlier, after he was captured. I thought this the most dramatic and deeply sad story I had heard, so I wrote in the briefing packet that Terry Anderson's wife had a daughter after he was taken hostage. In fact, Terry Anderson and his daughter's mother were not married at the time (they are now, by the way). Ted knew this, because he knew Terry Anderson. Ted called me later that night and said, "Terry Anderson was a well-known journalist in the Middle East. How can I trust the rest of your research if this simple fact is wrong?" And he was right. He was fair, but I was terribly embarrassed. Of course, it's hard to have your boss call you up and tell you that you screwed up, but this just made me more determined to check every fact for accuracy. You can't assume anything when you're researching and reporting.

One time, one of the facts I had gathered was called into question, but it turned out that I *was* right. It was a frustrating evening. We were going to do a story on the McMartin preschool case, involving multiple charges of child sexual molestation. The trial had been going on for several years, and it was extremely complicated. It was coming to an end, so we were preparing for the story, which I had researched so long and so hard that I really felt I knew it inside out. I was really proud of having learned it so well, because people had been covering it for years, and I had to become an expert in a few days. You could have awakened me in the middle of the night, and I could've remembered how many witnesses the prosecution called—I think 173—how many days the children were on the stand, all the details we might want to use to illustrate how harrowing this trial had been.

That day, Ted called me in and asked about the fact that some of the kids had been called to the stand and cross-examined during the pretrial hearing, which had gone on for quite a while. He said, "It's my understanding you don't do cross-examinations during a pretrial hearing." And I was positive that you do. I called one of the lawyers and said, "I know we went over this several times, but just to be sure, were the witnesses who were called during the pretrial hearing cross-examined?" and he replied, "Yes, in California we do have that law, but in most states"—including Maryland, where Ted's from—"you don't." I was glad to be called on something and be right.

I never got a chance to tell Ted, however, because five minutes later, about an hour before the show, someone rushed in and said, "Marion Barry has just been arrested for doing cocaine!" Frenzy set in as we dropped the McMartin story and switched to the one on Barry. We often changed the topic of the show the same day, but not usually at ten at night. I missed my chance to tell Ted I was right.

Looking back on my first year in television—only a few years ago, after all—I primarily recall the deep satisfaction of knowing that I was finally working in a place that felt right for me. I found coming to work each day both challenging and inspiring. I still feel that way and hope I always will.

Sara Just is now an associate producer with ABC News Nightline in Washington, D.C.

8

As Much Pizza as We Could Eat

GEORGE FLANIGEN

I first got interested in film when I was fifteen years old. I got on my first set in *W.W. & The Dixie Dancekings*, when Burt Reynolds did that movie here in Nashville. My brother had a car that they were using in it, and my mother talked to one of the contacts and said, "I've got a fifteen-year-old son who would like to come and watch." And he said, "Well, cool, bring him along; he can be an extra." So the movie crew cut my hair, put me in wardrobe, and I was an extra.

That was kind of the forerunner. Every time a movie was shot in town, I would get a call to come work as a general extra. After seeing the workings of the stages and sets, instead of being an extra who would go and sit in a room for four hours, I'd sneak out and go stand on set, and actually work on it if I could. I became a set brat, and I'd show up even when I wasn't on call.

From then on, it was my secret desire to go into film, but I decided I had to get my business degree and deal with this when I got out of college. My family is pretty conservative, and no one in it has ever wished or dreamed or wanted to be in the film industry, and they all kept telling me, "Film's kind of a hokey thing, and you can't get there from here." (Tennessee, in general, was not considered the most likely place to launch a movie career.) I really started to believe that. I had a guidance counselor at Memphis State who believed in me, but he believed my family more and told me, "Well, you're a business-type person." Every semester, I kept going back and asking, "Is there a film class?" and he'd say, "Maybe later." But by junior year, I had most of my business classes out of the way, and I started taking all my electives in the film department.

Well, from that point on, things got complicated.

A lot of my friends were marketing majors, business majors, management majors. They all were being interviewed on campus, and even I was being solicited by Procter & Gamble and other firms. All the big corporations hit campus, and if you're a sharp person and you've done a lot of good work in school and you have a good grade-point average, you can get a job before you graduate—and many of my friends did. But I didn't interview with any of those firms because I knew I wanted to work in the film industry.

It was 1981, and I wasn't sure which route I wanted to take. I knew that at this point the Nashville Network was starting up; I knew that there was a big production house here—Scene III—and that there was a film house as well. There seemed to be a lot of production going on and a lot of TV stations.

I thought, "I'm getting out with a good grade-point average. I have a really good résumé. I was in student government, and I did all the honor clubs and extracurricular stuff they tell you to do to make your résumé look great." Next to some of my friends in marketing and management, I thought, "Wow, I'm doing good."

So I get back to Nashville and start looking up all these places and sending out my résumé. I *blanket* the town with my résumé.

And maybe two letters came back—and they were Thank-you-but-no-thank-yous. I didn't even hear from the rest of them.

I had a good friend I went to high school with whose father was well connected in town, and through him I managed to get three to five interviews with people who were very gracious, and who gave me an inkling of what to expect. They told me it's tough to get into this field, and that I should be tenacious. That gave me some encouragement, and I started making phone calls and knocking on doors, but I was not very good at it. I did not like making those phone calls; I didn't like knocking on those doors. I did the best I could, but nothing seemed to work out. I hated it. I hated it because I always felt as if I was bugging people who were too busy to be talking to me anyway.

So I ended up changing my résumé half a dozen times and sent it out again, and about four months went by. It was terrible. I had planned for a difficult job search, but I never thought that it would be as tough as it was. I thought I would be somewhat marketable to employers, but that just wasn't the case. The problem with production is that if you don't really know what you're doing, you won't get hired. And it's very hard to get a job when you don't have any experience. But very few people are willing to give you that experience, and even fewer are willing to *pay* you to get that experience.

I had never edited on videotape—I had edited only on film—so I didn't have a lot to offer. I decided I needed some video experience, which I got through a friend of mine who had a friend, who had *another* friend who had just gotten a job at a new studio being built here by Viacom Cablevision. It was a community-access studio, a three-camera studio that the company was going to equip and staff to let groups produce programming locally. It was there for whoever wanted to use it under a franchise agreement with the city. The friend of my friend said, "You ought to go down there; they're accepting internships from people who want to give their time away." So I went down there.

Well, I didn't know what I was getting into. But I didn't care, as long as it was a job and I could start working. I've always said there are three reasons to do a job: (1) if you're learning something new; (2) if it opens up a door to get somewhere else; or (3) if you're making a lot of money. If you can get all three, that's great, but any one of those is a reason to do a job in production. I was there getting a foot in the door and learning a lot, and I thought it would lead to something better.

As interns, we did everything. Literally, the place was so new that we were able to shoot videotape in the field, we were able to work on editing the shows ourselves, and we were lighting the shows ourselves. We had to be jacks-of-all-trades. If the guy who did lighting for shows suddenly called in sick, I had to light the show. It would take me all day, but I'd figure it out. It was a wonderful place to make mistakes because no one could touch me—I could make mistakes and not get fired because I wasn't being paid.

I averaged about forty to eighty hours a week on the job, and I kept up that pace for nearly four months. By then, I'd been out of school eight months, and I had just about had it up to here with being broke. I was still going out trying to get work, still beating on doors, and I was learning a great deal, but I was really sick of this situation. I was considering getting out of the field, saying to heck with all this. My family was telling me to get out. And my friends were saying, "You're nuts." I was seeing all my friends in their normal jobs with their company cars, and I was just dying. All I could say was, "I'm a *mumble mumble* camera operator *mumble mumble* local studio." "How much money?" "I'm not getting any money." Well, I just didn't want to talk about it.

One day at home, I had my résumés spread across the kitchen

table, and I was taking stock of who had called me back and who hadn't called me back, and I was completely fed up with the world. Then the phone rang. It was the vice president and dean of students at Memphis State, who had been a friend of mine because I had dealt with him through student government. He had been kind of a mentor.

He said, "How ya doing?" Boy, did I let him know how I was doing! I really did; I just whaled on this poor guy. He was so taken aback that at first all he could say was "Oh, my gosh." Then he told me, "Look, you're trying to get into a business that's not normal, that's abnormal, that's strange, that's hard. *Don't judge yourself by what other people are doing.* If this is a field that you love and you want to be in it, hang in there."

That was exactly what I needed to hear. I had been ready to bail out—and I think I would have—but two weeks later a camera position opened up at that studio, and I got hired on as a camera operator. It was my first job in the industry—my first paying job. From that point on, I was able to eat and make ends meet.

Given the current job market, getting a first job eight months out of school doesn't sound that bad. Now there are kids in business and marketing who aren't even getting picked up out of school. So kids with broadcast degrees and communications goals probably have twice as long to wait for a job. It's probably getting tougher all the time. I believe the new graduates are coming out the same way we came out: clueless about what to expect.

Today, I tell students that there are a lot of people in the field of film who like to give others a break. Nobody got into this industry without somebody cracking open a door. In my case, the door was cracked open when a friend of a friend told me, "I've got a friend at this studio; go down and give your time away"— and even that wasn't easy. If someone tells you that he or she didn't have anyone's help, I think that person is lying.

I love this profession because it's a team sport. You have to cooperate with a group of people to get something done, and sometimes you accomplish the impossible. When you look at the final product, you think, "Wow, this went from an idea in the mind, to a piece of paper, to a group of people figuring out how to bring it to the screen, to a finished piece." At Viacom, our pieces were on the folk art fair at Centennial Park, on the jazz festival, on *anything* going on that we could pick up from the newspaper.

I liked to do the editing on my own, for I found I could learn from my own mistakes, and I'd learn things much faster that way. At most stations I couldn't have done that, because editors are often unionized and they're the only ones allowed to do that job. Instead of saying, "I wish that camera person had held that shot for ten seconds," I'd say, "I wish *I* had held that shot for ten seconds," or "I forgot the wide shot," or "I forgot to get the person walking away." It might take me ten hours to do that piece, but I'd learn that had I done it right, it would have taken only three.

Although I was officially called a local origination technician, I was mostly a camera operator, both in the studio and on location. I was learning how to shoot, but in the studio I could really do as much as I wanted. If I didn't know how to do something, I would stand over somebody who was doing it. (Even when I was off the payroll, I'd stick around longer and learn the next job.) That's how I learned to use the editing machine. In time, I'd stick tapes in and edit projects, and eventually some of those were put on the air.

I can remember the first piece I decided to do: on a fifties car show and car swap. I approached some of my friends who were working at the studio as techs and who loved cars as much as I did, and I said, "Why don't we go produce a show on our own?"

I persuaded my superiors at the studio to let us use the equipment, and we went out and produced a thirty-minute show, and put music down and all these cuts and interviews and so forth. My bosses loved it and aired it.

Well, they started giving me all these special projects, and before long I just climbed the ladder. I went from being a technician and a camera operator to an assistant producer. Then I directed some shows, and then I went all the way up to producer of the entire department.

That was my first paid year in TV, but my first year working with *film* in television began when I got to be good enough to start freelancing, about one year after that, in late 1983. I began working for a lot of different companies as a photographer and as a director, working nights, weekends, vacations. I had no personal life. That's how I met my current video production partner, Robert Deaton, on a freelance job. He was a camera operator, and so was I. We sat around and watched people running these projects and thought, "Maybe we can do this. Maybe we can do this better." People started calling Robert to do jobs and he would call me to help him out, and vice versa. We decided to form a company.

We worked probably eighteen hours a day, seven days a week for one solid year, from 1984 to 1985. Our company consisted of two beepers, an answering service, Robert, myself, and a girl-Friday in a small downstairs office off Third Avenue. We shared one desk and played musical chairs. We changed our lifestyles totally. We were starting over again. We sold everything we had, took every dollar we made on outside projects, and put it into an account.

While most people's idea of fun would be to go to a movie with friends or to a bar to hang out, fun for us—and this might sound silly and sick—would be to go meet a client after supper, set up four cameras and a truck, shoot till midnight, tear down, then go to some all-night pizza place. That's how our clients paid us: As much pizza as we could eat. We did so many jobs for pizza, it was not even funny.

Here we were starting over again, and I cannot tell you how many people told us we would never survive, that we couldn't compete with the East Coast or the West Coast companies. But in the mid-1980s, the video craze faded, and film took its place. With Robert's still-camera background and my film background, all of a sudden we were able to get projects. We went into business at the right time. A year later we had enough money to leave our jobs and do nothing but concentrate on that company.

The following is another first-year story: Our first music video job revolved around singer Sandi Patti. We were to shoot two music videos and a documentary as Patti made a nine-day journey in Israel. We said we would do the work on film, rather than video, and that was acceptable to the client.

Well, we got to Israel—and this is nuts, thinking of it now—but we had never used the camera that we took over there; it was brand new. And literally the night before the first shoot, Robert and I passed the manual back and forth between us, and we quizzed each other the next morning at breakfast. But we knew we could operate the camera if we studied and learned. And we got through the job and created some very nice pieces.

There were many first years, and to be honest with you, those first years are the same for everybody. That's why I'm so eager to talk about them. I go through first years all the time. There was the first year we went after the Christian music video market. Then we had another first year in the commercial market, when we started doing commercials. We had another first year when commercials dried up and we broke into country music videos, about three years ago, and then again trying to break into the West Coast market.

I don't think those first years ever stop. They're painful a lot of times, and you get a lot of rejection. Based on my own experiences, I offer the following advice: If you can live without this type of work, get the heck out, because you can do a lot better—more jobs, more personal time, more money—outside the field. But if you can't live without it, don't worry; you'll make enough money to survive. And if you're really good and you stick with it, one day you may turn around and realize you're doing pretty well. But you know, that's true with any endeavor.

> *George Flanigen is an award-winning music video and commercial producer, based in Nashville. He and partner Robert Deaton have their own company, Deaton Flanigen Productions, whose list of credits includes videos for Willie Nelson, Waylon Jennings, Clint Black, Vern Gosdin, and Paul Overstreet. Their video for Ricky Van Shelton won a gold record, selling 500,000 copies. Their commercial for the L.A. Lakers won a Los Angeles Emmy, one of the most prestigious awards in the business.*
>
> *Flanigen graduated from Memphis State University with a degree in business and a minor in film.*

9

Putting Emotions on Hold

SHERRY MARGOLIS

I had always dreamed of going into news, but I never thought I would do it. It's such a competitive field: It's like dreaming of being a major-league ballplayer. As a student, I was interested in journalism in general: I was editor of my high school paper, and I wrote for my college paper. I also wrote a column during high school for the local paper, about high school activities. I was always interested in writing, but at the time I thought I would be an English teacher, and I got my teaching certificate when I graduated. But there were no teaching jobs when I graduated, so I had to fall back on a television career!

My first job out of college was hosting and producing a daily children's program on a cable station in Buffalo. It was called the "Jelly Roll Review." I think the intended word was "Revue," like a musical revue, but the station somehow spelled it "review," as in review your notes, which meant nothing. The station had created this show, and I heard that it was looking for a host, so I auditioned for the job along with hundreds of other people. As the staff narrowed down the finalists, I kept making the cut, until finally there were three of us. They decided to give each of us a month on the air and then make their decision based on audience response. There was a lot of pressure, and potential for public humiliation—in a big way! I never heard what the viewer response was, exactly, but fortunately I got the job.

The show aired mornings, five days a week, but we taped all five shows on Fridays. I was on in segments, introducing the "Addams Family," "The Partridge Family"—both as syndicated reruns—and the "Bullwinkle" cartoon show. In all I was on the air for about fifteen minutes, and I was to do whatever I could come up with. We had a budget of ten dollars a week, which came to two dollars a show! There were no children, no puppets, no goldfish; there was nothing! There was a stool, this strange logo for "Jelly Roll Review," and me! My talents were limited: I'm not a great cook, and I don't play an instrument. Nevertheless, I came up with some rather creative ideas, and my mother even helped me with some of them. I did sandpainting a few times. Tuesday was "Jelly Roll Reviews the News," when I would read news items that were relevant to children, along with letters from children who had also sent in pictures they had drawn. Once a week we had "Mystery Tour," and we would "visit" a different country or a different period in history. One time I contacted the Japanese social club in Buffalo, which gave me Japanese food and music and clothing, and we talked about Japan. One time the Buffalo Historical Museum allowed me to use a butter churn and other early American tools, and I talked about that period in history. Then I ran out of ideas, and I decided to get some guests. I had professional athletes show us how to dribble basketballs, for example; I had professional musicians come on and teach us songs. If a school group was performing a musical, I would have them come on and perform one of the songs. I had police officers and firefighters.

Although it sounds like a silly job that had nothing to do with journalism, I learned skills in that job that I still use today. I was responsible for producing these shows, so I learned how to produce. I also learned how to interview people, which I hadn't had a lot of experience doing. The job taught me some other basic skills that came in handy later in my career.

The position lasted only a few months. That's because the station was sold and lost all its programming, including my show. I worked for a while as an editorial assistant for a magazine and then was accepted into the graduate program in communication at the State University of New York at Buffalo.

While I was in graduate school, I got a job in radio news for one of the top radio stations in town. While doing that job, I was approached by the news director of the ABC TV affiliate in Buffalo, which was the sister station of the radio station and was owned by the same company. He had heard me on the radio and was sufficiently impressed to call me. He said he liked my style on the air, and he hired me to do part-time reporting. I was holding two jobs. I would run to the TV station every morning to do the morning cut-ins (local news breaks in a network show) during "Good Morning America." When I finished there, I would go to the radio station to do my radio job. On my days off from the radio job, I reported for the TV station, learning how to do television reporting. For a while, I was working seven days a week, but I loved it, and when you're young, you have the energy to do these things. Buffalo was a fairly large TV market to start out in, and this was a lucky break for me.

TV was completely different from radio. I was not used to worrying about the pictures to go along with the words, and worrying about my on-camera presence. For one thing, I had to buy a whole wardrobe—I had a radio wardrobe, which is to say no wardrobe at all! I suddenly started worrying about all these cosmetic concerns—clothes, hair, and makeup. But on a more serious note, I had to learn about the technical aspects of television, and how to get the video to go along with the copy. I caught on pretty quickly, and I loved the work. I loved radio as well—in a sense there's less bull: You cut to the chase, you don't have to worry about the pictures or your hair, and if you have a breaking story you can get the information and get right on the air with it. We've reached a point in television, however, where we have the technology to do that too—but you still have to worry about your hair and makeup. In radio, there are also fewer people and less equipment: You have your notepad, and you get the story, you write it, and you go on the air with it. You turn your microphone on and off yourself. It's just you and the microphone, and you're responsible for the entire process, and there's something very satisfying about that. In television you're responsible for a good part of it, but there are people to do the technical work, a director, a producer, and so on.

The story that I remember most vividly from that first year happened when I hadn't been working at the TV station very long. A call came in: There had been an accident with fatalities. It was in a town that was some distance from Buffalo. It involved some college students—three girls and three boys—and the roads were rain-slicked. These six college friends had been traveling to town together, they had all been part of the homecoming court, they had all been outstanding as seniors, and they were all killed. I'll never forget working on that story. It was one of the real tests that I had to go through. When we arrived at the scene, the bodies hadn't even been recovered yet, and it was raining, and the whole mood was very somber. I looked for the car, and I couldn't see it. People pointed, and there was a mangled mass of what had once been a subcompact car, twisted around a tree. That's what was left. It was a long, excruciating process removing the bodies with the "jaws of life." It was horrible being on the scene for that. Then I had to go to the college, because I had to get information about these students. I really surprised myself: I talked to some students, who had not yet heard the news, and I had to break it to them. I realized I should get pictures of the victims, so I somehow tracked down a yearbook that included all their portraits. We got back to the station, where we had to wait while, one by one, the families of the victims were notified before we could release their names on the air. The entire process was painful, but I surprised myself by being able to get through it and put the story together, and stay rational the whole time. I think we were the only station that had the victims' pictures, and because my news director was working closely with me, we were the only station that had all six names by airtime.

The story got on the air, and then I collapsed. I went into the ladies' room and just cried, and I remember looking in the mirror and seeing I was white as a ghost. I went back to my desk, still very shaken, and the assistant news director came up to me—he was a very nice man—he put his hand on my shoulder, and he asked me how I was. I said that I was okay and was glad that I had gotten the story on the air. I apologized that I was being so emotional about it, because I was still a neophyte and I assumed that to be a newsperson, you had to have this hard edge, and that you shouldn't let stories like this get to you. I was a little embarrassed that this story had gotten to me so much. So I said to him, "Well, I guess the next time will be easier," and he said, "I hope not," which was a very tender, sweet thing to say. He meant that if it becomes easier, you become less of a feeling person, and you don't have to do that to be a newsperson. I was proud of myself, because I am a very emotional person, and I still find it difficult to report stories like that. But that first experience was a test to see whether I could put my emotions on hold long enough to get the job done, and I was able to do so. You don't have to stop feeling, but you have to distance yourself at least until the job is done. It's like being a physician, or any other profession that involves human tragedy; you have to finish the job first, then allow yourself the luxury of feeling the pain.

I've never had an anchoring job where I didn't write for the show, and I like writing. I like the direct communication I have with the audience. I enjoy that and am good at it, and I find it rewarding. I have some background in theater, and in a way being an anchor is performing, so it really combines all my interests and talents.

It was helpful to me to start in radio, and many of the people I work with now started in radio, too. I think that's a viable option if there are few jobs available in television. I would also encourage people to start out in smaller markets than I did, because I learned in front of more people than I would have in, for example, Marquette, Michigan, and so I made mistakes in front of more people. Moreover, since Buffalo was my hometown, I made my mistakes in a very public way in front of all these people I knew. If you go to a small market, you're learning and making mistakes in front of strangers, and just a small number of strangers at that. You'll also get more hands-on experience at a smaller market. In Buffalo the union regulations prevented me from shooting and editing tape, but in a smaller city, you can get invaluable experience in shooting and writing and editing.

I was at that station for about three years, and then I came to Detroit, where I was hired as an anchor and reporter. When college students ask me now for tips on how to get into television, I recommend that they do an internship. For one thing, some people may find the environment of a newsroom unpleasant. There's a lot of stress, a lot of noise, a lot of static, people racing tapes down the hall and screaming at each other, police radios blaring.

Some people don't really know, until they get there, what the TV news environment is all about. All they know is what they *see* on television. Also, it's a direct experience that you can put on your résumé, and you can actually watch the reporters interviewing people and putting their stories together, and see how things work. Once you're a reporter, you have to learn how to think on your feet, to recognize at a moment's notice the shots that you're going to need, and the interviews that you'll need, and the angle of the story, and then write in the car as you're racing back to the station to meet that deadline: You have to learn how to do all that and learn it quickly. It's invaluable experience.

Sherry Margolis is an anchor at WJBK-TV, the CBS affiliate in Detroit. She earned a bachelor's degree in English and did graduate work in communication at the State University of New York at Buffalo.

10

The Scriptless Weather Girl

LAURA FABER

I knew since high school that I wanted to work in television. At first I was interested in behind-the-scenes kinds of things. The summer before my last semester at Michigan State University, majoring in telecommunications, I did my first internship, at WXYZ-TV Channel 7 in Detroit. I started work in the production department and was involved in "Kelly & Co." and "Good Morning America." But "Good Morning America" was canceled by my local station about two weeks after my arrival, so the station had to place ten college interns in other jobs. The interns could choose which department they wanted to go to, and I decided to work in news, specifically with the reporter who does consumer advocate news, Charlotte Scott.

I loved it. I loved news. I especially liked the storytelling part of it, and I also enjoyed the idea of helping people with consumer reporting. I was lucky, because I was in one of the few internships that really allowed us to do a lot of work. Channel 7 was a union station, so we were not allowed to edit or touch the equipment or shoot anything. But what we could do—at least with the consumer reporter—was get on the phone and talk to people. She let us come up with the story ideas, research them, and set up all the interviews, and then we would give her all the questions so that she would just go into the story with our packet of information. That way we were able to write our own version of the story to send with our résumés for job interviews. Charlotte was wonderful because she gave us a lot of leeway to do much of her job.

After working in the newsroom, I absolutely had the bug: I wanted a career in TV, even though I had thought I'd stay behind the scenes. I probably got caught up in the glamour of it, even though I'm not sure that the job really was glamorous—but how many times does a college-student intern get to take a helicopter ride to do a story in Lansing, Michigan, the state capital? I really liked that. It was also glamorous to not sit at a desk eight hours a day, to spend every day meeting new people. All these things convinced me I wanted to be in news reporting.

Now I tell people interested in TV careers to investigate internships more than I did, to make sure they'll really get something to do, and not just sit and watch. I stayed in Detroit because I grew up there and I was going to be living at home, but it was really too big a city to offer internships involving real work, real reporting. I just happened to get lucky and be with a reporter who let the interns do more.

After I graduated from college, I began looking for jobs not only in television but in public relations, because I wasn't sure how long it was going to take me to find a job in television. One of my friends had gotten a job with Tony Franco, a PR firm in Detroit. She got me an interview, and about two weeks after graduation the company offered me a job. I was supposed to start two weeks later. In the meantime, I had made a résumé tape at Channel 7, but copying such tapes is expensive, so I was also sending out written résumés to TV stations, along with a photo of myself and a cover letter saying, "Listen, I'm a brand-new college graduate, and I don't have thousands of tapes. If you're interested, let me know and I'll send you one." I actually got a couple of good responses, from Duluth, Minnesota, from La Crosse, Wisconsin, other places in the Midwest, and from Salinas, California. I looked only at market sizes smaller than the top one hundred markets—tiny, tiny towns—thinking that with no experience, that was where I would get a job.

A TV station in La Crosse, Wisconsin, wanted to interview me to do the weekend weather. I had to pay my way out there for an audition. I'd never done the weather, and I was scared to death because I did not know what the hell I was doing. I brought all these maps with me on the twelve-hour train ride out there so I at least knew where all the states were! Actually, I already knew the location of most of them, but I just wanted to practice and it was the only thing I could think of to prepare.

My studying must have worked, because the station offered me the job of weekend "weather girl" and general assignment reporter, working on weekends and three days during the week. So I called Franco and quit my job—even though I hadn't even started it yet. I said, "TV is what I really want to do. I apologize, but I really need to do this."

Everybody told me—that is, all my parents' friends told me—television was not a good business to be in. It was terrible for family life, it wasn't stable, nothing was guaranteed, on and on. So I told myself, "Okay, I've always wanted to do this, so I'm going to try it. I'm going to give myself five years, and if I have not been able to move up to a decent-sized market I'm going to do something else and get out of the business, because no way am I going to be in Boise, Idaho"—although I'm sure it's a lovely town—"when I'm thirty-six and still trying to make it!"

My parents, however, were definitely supportive; they wanted me to do whatever I wanted to do. And thank God, because my first salary was rock bottom, and they helped me financially.

All that job searching took a total of one month, and to get a first job in television in one month is unbelievable. I had anticipated it might take six months to a year. People in Detroit told me it could take a long time, and the other people I had interned with were finding it was taking them a while. But one thing I'm convinced helped me—and I still say to students to this day—is that the best time to look for a job is in the first quarter of the year. That's when I've gotten all my jobs. I'm convinced that at New Year's, people have new attitudes: It's after they do budgets; it's after the holidays and into a new year. I'm convinced that had something to do with it.

I packed up, moved to La Crosse, Wisconsin, and did the weather. And I turned out to be pretty good at it, which eventually became a problem because I didn't particularly want to be the weather girl; I wanted to do news. I was good because I didn't have any problems memorizing the weather report very quickly before each news broadcast and then talking about it on the air for four minutes without a script. I also didn't have a problem with being a little bit of a ham on the air, which made viewers like me.

Although I didn't particularly care about doing the weather, I did care enough to do a good job and get all my facts straight. In the process, I learned a lot about live, on-camera reporting. Today, at my current job in Nashville, I don't do very many live shots, but at my second job, in Minnesota, I did them all the time. On a live shot, you have to ad-lib, and doing the weather definitely helped me learn to ad-lib because I was up there before the camera for four minutes with no script. If there were big storms across the country, watches or warnings, I would have some notes with me, but otherwise, nothing. The experience was great in helping me be myself on the air.

I'm so grateful to that news director who first hired me, because I looked at my first résumé tape recently, and of course it's awful, and I wonder why in the world he would have hired me. As I said earlier, because my internship was at a union station I was not allowed to edit there, so I did not know how to do any editing once I got to my first job—and editing is essential in this business. I hung out with the weather guy for the first day, and tried to learn how to edit, but when I was sent out on my first story—it was about a rural grocery store that was about to shut down, and the owners were trying to save it by holding a fund-raiser—it took me something like three hours to edit my first news package—way too long. Thank God, it was a story that happened early in the morning, and somehow I managed to edit it before airtime. But this was baptism by fire. I don't recommend learning to edit the very day you need to complete a story.

La Crosse is a college town, so for someone fresh out of college it was a fun place to be. It is located in a beautiful part of the state, right on the Mississippi River with lots of bluffs. Everybody else at work was single and about my age, and we all hung out together and there was a lot of camaraderie.

That's one of the good things about a small market, which I think you definitely don't have in a large metropolitan area. By the time they get to bigger markets, people have been in the business so long that they have bigger egos, and they aren't as willing to help you because you should know what you're doing by then. I think it's best to begin in a small market, where you get a lot of support from your peers because they are all in exactly the same boat you are.

Of course, I made mistakes on my first job. It's frustrating, because once you make them, there's not much you can do. You want to be accurate 100 percent of the time, and it's not going to happen, because you're only human. My most unforgettable mistake concerned two stories I had for the evening news. One was a painful school board meeting, and the other one was the circus that was in town. First I covered the school board meeting, which may have been about raising property taxes, and which had lots of angry parents and the superintendent defending his position. Then we had to go by the circus and interview a clown. I got back late, I was rushed—it was the first time I felt real deadline pressure. I wrote the two stories, edited my own tapes, and gave them to the tape operator minutes before we hit the air. We led the broadcast with the school board story, and instead of the superintendent, up comes a photo of the circus clown behind the anchor. I tell you, I was so embarrassed, and I was chewed out by the anchors and the news director, and I felt awful. I just said, "You're right; I did it; I made a mistake." I think they were shocked that I admitted it so quickly, because for some reason in this business people have a tendency to point fingers and never to take the blame themselves. Afterward because it was so obvious I had made the mistake, people kind of backed off and the crisis was over. Today, I still try to meet my mistakes head-on: If I've really, truly made a mistake, I make sure that I own up to it. People are much more forgiving that way and give you credit if you're honest.

I had good packages that first year, but no undercover, investigative exposés. One thing I was proud of, though, was a story I broke on the Company Store, a direct-mail company that sells comforters and bedding and is headquartered in La Crosse, where it was a major employer. There was a rumor that the president would be laying off hundreds of people, but he kept refusing to comment on it. I called him and asked if I could interview him about something else, a new product he was adding to the catalog and whether he thought it would fly. He agreed to the interview, and while I was there, I said, "Okay, Terry, I have to ask you this: What about the layoffs?" And he answered! So we were the only station to have that story, and of course we made it the first item in the newscast. He ended up having a news conference about it the next day because so many other news stations and newspapers were hounding him on it. That was the greatest thing, when I got that coup.

In La Crosse, I had to get used to living in a fishbowl. It's a much bigger fishbowl in Nashville, where I am now, but people in a tiny rural town may feel they know you even better than they do in midsized cities. Thus can be difficult, but it's something I've had to learn to deal with. People are always going to approach you because you're in their living rooms every night, and they think they have a right to tell you what they think of you. They're always really nice, but it's different from being just an average citizen.

The first time I noticed this phenomenon, I was in a grocery store in La Crosse on one of my days off, and I was wearing sweats and no makeup. Someone came up to me and said, "Oh, it's the weather lady from Channel 8! Hi!" And that person looked me up and down and surmised, "You must not be working today." You get that all the time, people who say, "You look so much better in person"; "You look so much thinner in person." They really mean it as a compliment, but it's very weird when people call you at the station to say, "Those earrings are terrible on you"; "That color is great for you, you need to wear it more often"; "You need to wear your hair back." It's like having thousands of mothers out there watching you.

I also learned in La Crosse that news directors are not always going to look out for your best interests. I was passed over for anchor jobs, and Monday-through-Friday general assignment jobs—jobs they knew I wanted—because they thought I was good

The Scriptless Weather Girl

at the weather and should stay with it. That became discouraging personally, and frustrating professionally because I was not being taken seriously. During the week, for instance, while I was on general assignment, I covered a news conference on a big homicide. All the reporters from around town were there, and the chief of police said, "Okay, is everybody here? Yes, we have the papers, people from Channel 19, the *weather lady* from 8 . . ." I thought, "This is totally ruining my credibility as a reporter. It's driving me nuts." I learned that people weren't going to be looking out for me, that I had to make my future happen, and that meant I had to start looking for another job.

I started my next job in Rochester, Minnesota, after working at Channel 8 for thirteen months. Rochester was really a lateral move in terms of market size, but it was a place where I knew I could get more responsibility. I started out as a weekend reporter. Shortly thereafter, I started doing morning cut-ins—news teases featuring the stories coming up on the show that day—and anchoring. I discovered that I really liked anchoring, and that I wanted to pursue it. About five months later, the woman who coanchored the five o'clock news left, so I started coanchoring, and about a year after that, I was anchoring both the five and the six o'clock news. Of course, I was doing a lot of other things for the show, because Rochester is still a really small market. I did everything from producing the whole show, to lining up the guests—we had live guests—to writing everything, to editing everything, plus doing a news report.

If you want to work in television news, I recommend that you go to a small market, and not be ashamed of it, because that's where you're going to learn to do everything. That's where you learn to be grateful when you get to larger markets like Nashville, and you don't have to do everything anymore—the shooting and the editing and the producing and the odd jobs—because the staffs are so much bigger. I've met people here who have worked only in Nashville, and they complain if they have to do something extra. I look at them and say, "You know, you need to go to a tiny market, like number 140 in size, and see how much extra work you have to do."

I'm happy about what I consider to be my success, and my ability to continue to move up and do what I want to do, which is anchor. Good things have happened to me, and I believe that it's because I've worked really hard to make them happen, I've been honest and made sure that I've done my job; I've always been receptive to criticism; I've always asked for help if I really needed it. I tell students: The best thing that you can do is take classes in public policy or political science, and classes in which you can do a lot of public speaking, not just classes in journalism. And read, read, read.

In Rochester, when I started coanchoring the five o'clock news, it was the number-three show, and within two ratings periods it went to number one. That was one of my proudest achievements there. In Nashville, I have been proudest of a documentary I did about health insurance and the middle class. It was nominated for an Emmy and received a regional Green Eyeshade Award from the Radio, Television News Directors Association, and a national Iris Award.

Laura Faber is anchor for the morning news program "Scene at Sunrise" for WSMV-TV Channel 4 in Nashville, Tennessee.

11

The Chair Behind the Anchor's Chair

ALISON CRAIGLOW

I knew while I was at Barnard College of Columbia University that I wanted to be a journalist, but I wanted to be a print journalist. I'd always wanted to be a writer, and ever since I was little, my family read a lot of newspapers, and politics and other current affairs issues were important in my family. I had an internship at a children's magazine when I was a freshman in college, and I was the Columbia University stringer for the *New York Times* during college, pitching story ideas and helping the paper with larger stories on higher education—I also got to write two or three full articles. It was good money, and it was a great experience, but I spent only one day per week at the newspaper office, so I never actually felt like part of the staff. I was also a staff reporter for the Columbia daily student newspaper, the *Spectator,* for three years, and I was the publisher my senior year.

Before I graduated, I decided I didn't want to move to a small town, so I started applying for jobs in various cities. Since I knew that recent graduates stand a very slim chance of getting a job at a paper in a big city, I applied for jobs at CNN in Washington and at ABC News in New York. I felt excited about TV work, but in some ways I was also apprehensive that I was going into a field that didn't have as much integrity and depth as print. I still have conflicting feelings about this sometimes. Nevertheless, I needed a job, and I think I was also a little bit scared of writing; I knew I was a good writer for a college paper, but I was scared of trying to do the job in the real world, trying to make deadlines every day. I thought that in television, the pressure wouldn't be so much on me alone, which was definitely the case: Television is a collaborative field. Making the deadline in TV depends on a lot of different factors and people.

The ABC interview for a desk assistant's job was tough. I was asked what my skills were as a journalist, why I wanted to be in television—that question I had to fudge—which newspapers I read and how I read them—did I read the home section first, or the front page first? Although the interview was tough, I felt quite good about it, because the skills I got from the *Spectator* were pretty incredible.

It took about three months to get an answer about a position, even though I kept calling and nagging the network. The day before graduation—when I still had no idea what I was going to do—I was finally offered a job as desk assistant. I said, "Great! Can I start in August?"—I wanted to bum around awhile. The reply: "No. You can start next week. Take it or leave it." I took it!

Desk assistant jobs were very low paying and miserable. I worked from four in the afternoon to midnight and on weekends; my yearly salary was $17,000 or $18,000. In New York City, that's not much. I did a lot of answering phones, a lot of copying, and a lot of faxing. But I was sitting in the newsroom where all the news comes in first from around the world, and I learned so much through osmosis that I can't even begin to quantify it. Compared to people who didn't have experience on a daily college newspaper, I found I was much more efficient and resourceful. I could streamline my thoughts and get right down to what needed to be done. Those skills are invaluable. I get calls from people at my college all the time, and I tell them, if you still have time to do it, work for your daily campus paper, because there's nothing like it.

On my first day at ABC, I walked into the newsroom that you see behind Peter Jennings's anchor desk, and I was overwhelmed. I was told the chair I was to sit in was directly behind the anchor chair. It was all very glamorous and exciting. That feeling quickly dissipated, but the first week was thrilling, watching the program get put together and having access to so much information.

After a week, reality started kicking in, and I realized the job wasn't remotely as challenging as college or working on the campus paper. I felt as if my brain was going to turn into mush. I wasn't aware at the time of all the information I was absorbing being there. If I had known it then, I wouldn't have gotten so frustrated so quickly.

I had various responsibilities. I distributed daily lists of where each staff member had been assigned for the day. Each afternoon I had to attend the five-thirty meeting in which all the bureau chiefs got on the phone and talked about what was to be covered the next day. I had to write up notes from that meeting and distribute them, which was also good experience. The other desk assistants and I had to watch the two other network news broadcasts and type up a log of their stories to send to everybody on the staff. One of the best duties was picking out the ten-second video for the forty-five-second news brief. I would get the script of a particular news story and find out how many seconds the story ran, then go through the videotape of whatever the event was—say, then President Bush signing some piece of legislation—and I would pick out the best ten seconds of tape. I know now that that was a really good exercise, because it was training me visually for television. Eventually, I went out with crews to shoot stories.

I learned everything it takes to put together a broadcast, which is so much more than it takes to put together a print news story. Not so much more work journalistically, but more logistically, with staff and equipment. I learned who the decision makers were and how decisions were made and why we covered things the way we did.

The year I was a desk assistant (1988) was an election year, and one of my jobs every day was to make phone calls to the Dukakis and Bush campaign headquarters to see if they had any new television advertisements coming out that we could incorporate into our stories. I was pretty good about keeping on top of this, but one day I called the Bush camp, and I said, "I heard you have a new ad coming out. Is that true?" The response was, "No, but call us back later." Well, I never called back later, because I got wrapped up in something. In fact, there was a new ad, and both of the other major networks had it, and ABC didn't. I knew I had blown it, and I was really scared. I can laugh at it now, but when Brit Hume, who was covering the Bush campaign at the time, yelled at me over the phone, I went into the bathroom and cried. Now I look back on the incident and think it was no big deal. But it was scary at the time. The competition is just like in print: If somebody else gets a story before you do, it's bad!

Experiences with the stars, in the beginning can be scary too, because you don't realize that they're real people. You think that they're bigger than life, and it's very intimidating. One time, Sam Donaldson was sitting in front of me, and he was asking—sort of shouting into the wind—"How soon do I have to get in a cab to make a six o'clock flight at LaGuardia?" I didn't answer him because I didn't think he was talking to me. He was on the phone, and he must have been on hold, but he wasn't looking at me. He shouted again, "When do I have to get in a cab?!?" He looked at me and said, "YOU! I'm talking to YOU!" *I* didn't know how long it takes to get to LaGuardia. I was only twenty-one years old; I'd never flown around the world. I was so startled! I said, "Uh, uh . . . ," and then I made something up. I hope he made his flight.

After a year and eight months I got promoted: That's a year and eight months of my brain getting mushy. I really thought I was going to lose my skills. That's a long time not to be writing. But the experience ended up better than I expected: now I could pitch story ideas and keep thinking journalistically, and I could make of it what I wanted.

I was promoted to production associate and joined the documentary unit. My responsibilities suddenly increased dramatically, and I was much more a part of the show. From there I was promoted to senior production associate for the "American Agenda" segments on "World News Tonight," and a year after that I became associate producer.

I'm still not sure about television. I feel there's a lot of pressure to get good ratings, and I don't always agree with what my bosses think will bring good ratings. Good ratings alone are not a very good goal if you're a journalist. I think we tend to cover very obvious, unchallenging news stories. In print, there are many more venues. If I were a print journalist, even if I had a wacky, radical story that I wanted to get published, I could find some sort of outlet for it. Television, on the other hand, is a very small world, and there aren't many alternatives. Still, I wouldn't be here if I didn't think we do a lot of good things on TV. It's such a powerful medium, and there are stories that just don't tell as well, that don't make an impression on people, in print as they do on television. Stories like the Berlin Wall coming down, or the uprising in China's Tiananmen Square—those are things that even the most brilliant writers would have had great difficulty capturing the way television did. Seeing the face of an AIDS victim in your living room, and hearing him tell you about his illness, is a powerful experience and can move you to do good things. And television is where a lot of people get their news.

The most obvious thing that makes working in television different from print is the collaborative aspect of television, and the fact that you don't have a beat. You get put on a variety of news stories, but you're always working in conjunction with three or four other people. In the end, I like the collaboration, but sometimes it's frustrating: There's a huge disproportion of neurotic people in television, and if you're working with someone very intensely, sometimes every day until five in the morning for a week, and you're not getting along, it's definitely a challenge. Television is also less gritty and less real; the people who work here are more elite, more wealthy, and less in touch with the real world and the people they cover than are the people who work in newspapers. That is frustrating. But just like print journalism, this medium can be very intellectually fulfilling, and the people I work with are intellectually stimulating. Working in TV takes a big personal toll, and your schedule is never your own. Weekends and vacations get ruined on a regular basis.

There's stiff competition for desk assistant jobs, but these days the networks have so many newsmagazine shows that there are more opportunities now than there were five years ago. It is tough to break into this business, but it pays to be persistent. At least that's what I've found.

> *Alison Craiglow is a production associate for the ABC News magazine show "Day One." She graduated from Barnard College of Columbia University with a major in American history.*

12
A One-Man Band in Fairbanks

Kelly Schnell Huotari

"Good morning. It's thirty-eight degrees below zero. I'm Kelly Schnell." Those were the first words I ever uttered on television.

Landing that first on-air TV news job is not easy. Persistence and determination are absolute requirements—and a little luck certainly doesn't hurt. Knowing this, I promised myself I would accept the first offer that came my way. Nine months into my job search, I got the call I had been waiting for. It came from the smallest and, without a doubt, the coldest market in the country: Fairbanks, Alaska. The station was KTVF, a combination NBC-CBS affiliate. Move over, Jane Pauley, I was on my way.

I caught the TV bug while I was a senior at the University of Washington in Seattle, majoring in international studies and economics. A classmate had just been hired for an entry-level position at a local TV station, and she talked about her new job incessantly. It wasn't long before I too was hooked. I finally knew what I wanted to do when it came time to take that plunge into the real world. As far as I was concerned, the news business had it all: the excitement of tight deadlines, cameras, and bright lights;

fascinating real-life stories; and best of all, the chance to "make a difference" by sharing important information with tens of thousands of viewers.

I quickly discovered that the majority of jobs in TV news call for a degree in broadcast journalism. Learning this, I feared I'd struck out before even getting up to the plate. But during informational interviews at local stations, I was assured that a broadcasting degree is not always a prerequisite for success and that I could actually be trained on the job. I got more encouragement from a Seattle news anchor, whom I met through a mutual friend. She told me that my international studies degree would prove to be a big plus when it came to understanding and writing about national and world events.

Perhaps the most important advice I received came in the form of a warning. I was told repeatedly that chasing a career in TV news requires a lot of sacrifice. In a nutshell: no pain, no gain. My lack of experience meant that initially, I would have no choice but to accept low-paying jobs. Also, I had to be willing to work anywhere in the country. This wasn't a time to be picky about geography.

Putting together a résumé videotape is the first step in applying for an on-air reporting or anchoring job. To that end, I pursued a minimum-wage desk assistant job at KOMO-TV, the Seattle ABC affiliate. I had learned about the job during a series of informational interviews with local station producers. In fact, one of the producers I had met at a competing station made a phone call for me and recommended me for the job. I was finally hired after an interview in which I agreed to work odd hours and promised to be available upon short notice.

Once inside the station, I was able to bribe the production crew (it only took a few pizzas) to let me sit on the news set and record some anchoring segments. On my days off, I tagged along with news crews in the field. In exchange for helping haul around heavy TV equipment to a shoot, the camera operators videotaped me doing stand-ups, as if I were actually reporting on the scene. After the actual story aired, I borrowed the field tapes for material to produce mock-up news reports with myself as reporter. Within a month I had a ten-minute résumé tape. I then subscribed to a national hot line (called Media Line) to find out about current openings in TV news around the country.

During the next six months, I sent out between five and ten résumé tapes a day, mostly to places I'd never even heard of like Glendive, Montana; Utica, New York; and Rock Springs, Wyoming. The competition was fierce. For every six-dollar-an-hour job that was advertised, there were usually several hundred applicants. Time passed and I became pretty discouraged. During one interview, in eastern Washington, I could hardly see the news director over the stacks of résumé tapes on his desk.

On the positive side, I used this time to start learning how to produce television news. I left KOMO and went to KING-TV, Seattle's NBC affiliate, for what is probably the most unglamorous job in television. My job title was grip (read "grunt"), which meant I strung cable, put up lights, and monitored audio levels. No job was too small. I fetched coffee and, on one occasion, I risked life and limb to chase a reporter's favorite pen down a steep hill. But the job did provide some excellent training. I accompanied news crews into the field daily, closely observing the reporters and photographers as they covered complex issues and human drama, condensing tragedy and triumph into one-and-a-half-minute stories.

Nine months afer deciding to become a TV reporter, I got the break I had been waiting for. The operations manager at KTVF in Fairbanks called and offered me a job as an anchor-reporter. She said my application stood out because of my experience assisting news crews in a large market. Most of the other candidates for the job had no paid work experience. I was told the job at KTVF paid $19,000 a year, take it or leave it. The salary sounded pretty good to me, because at the time I didn't know about Alaska's overinflated economy. Ten days later I was on a northbound jet, packed with rowdy oil workers intent on getting in one last round of double bourbons before reaching Alaska's North Slope.

Everything happened so fast that reality didn't sink in until I was standing in the Fairbanks Airport, surrounded by three big cardboard boxes full of all the pieces of my life. I suddenly realized I was 2,400 miles from home and didn't know a soul in the entire state.

A second realization hit as I headed out into the sunny March afternoon to hail a cab: It's darn cold in Alaska. Not just your usual run-of-the-mill, time-to-zip-up-your-coat cold, but bone-chilling cold. I quickly hopped into a cab and started trying to resuscitate my bloodless fingers and toes while the driver launched into a steady stream of chatter about the current warm spell. Apparently nine degrees below zero in March is nothing short of balmy to native Alaskans.

My first night in a motel in Fairbanks felt very long. However, before my alarm clock could do its job, the entire newsroom staff (a total of three other people) descended upon my room to wake me up. Although it was Sunday and technically everyone's day off, we were all assigned to cover an event that puts Fairbanks on the map every year: the North America Dogsled Championships.

My job was to shoot the dogsled teams as they raced across the Fairbanks Golf Course before heading out of town. I was given an ancient camera and a quick lesson on focusing and rolling videotape, and then I was on my own. I hunkered down in a big snowdrift and waited for what seemed like hours, most of which I spent wondering why I hadn't brought boots to Alaska. Then in a flash, a dog team burst out of a nearby stand of evergreens. In all my excitement I forgot to hit the roll button and completely missed capturing the event on videotape. But not to worry. I had plenty of other chances. For the next three hours I manned my post, taking pictures of several teams that whipped by in a flurry of white powder, paws flying and mushers barking orders.

I first set foot in the station at 4 A.M. the next morning. KTVF was located in the town's only high-rise. Eight stories high, the building appeared to be constructed out of scrap metal and looked like a tall, skinny Quonset hut. A bar took up most of the main floor. The smell of cigarettes and stale beer followed me to the elevator where a dusty sign, minus a few letters, informed me that I would find KTVF on the second floor.

Once upstairs, I was met in the news room by Scot, a fellow reporter, who had appointed himself the interim news director (the last news director had left several weeks earlier to take a job at the University of Alaska—Fairbanks. Finding a replacement was taking longer than expected). Scot had assumed the daunting task of training me. "Hi," he said, smiling. "Let's get going. You're on the air in two hours."

Gulp. "Me? I thought I was just training today," I answered feebly. As it turned out, Scot was of the learning-by-doing school. After hastily scanning the news wires, I sat down to write my scripts. I needed enough copy to fill a five-minute local "news hole" in the "Today" show. It's amazing how long five minutes can seem when the biggest news of the day, next to the dogsled race, is a small fire at the town's garbage dump.

The next thing I knew, I was seated at the orange Formica news set, in front of a backdrop covered in blue shag carpeting—leftovers from the seventies that hadn't aged well. The red tally light on the camera came on and the words came out of my mouth: "Good morning. It's thirty-eight degrees below zero." The rest is all a blur.

When it was over, Scot raced me down the hall to the station's radio studio. Before I knew it, I was once again sending news and information over the airwaves.

After three more TV and radio cut-ins, the real work of the day began. The other two reporters had arrived at the station by then, and the four of us sat down and began sifting through the wire copy and the local newspaper, the *Fairbanks Daily News Miner*, looking for stories to cover. Each of us was required to come up with a minimum of three stories each day.

After working the phones to set up the day's interviews and photo shoots, it was time to hit the road. Alone. Unlike bigger markets, reporters in small towns usually work as "one-man bands." That means doing double duty as both photographer and reporter on every story. I had to lug around heavy, third-rate camera equipment and take my own pictures, while making sure I got the facts straight and looked professional on camera.

What I lacked in experience, I made up in enthusiasm. The work was hard, but each story was an adventure. On that first Monday morning, I headed out the door to interview Russians who were building a mansion-sized ice sculpture down the street, as a show of goodwill toward the people of Fairbanks. The next stop was the animal research center, which was hosting an open house to show off baby musk ox and reindeer. When I arrived, the newborns were wobbling around in their pens, trying out their shaky legs for the first time.

Back at the station, I viewed my tapes and headed for the typewriter. I can still remember the thrill I felt, sitting down to write my first real field report. I was shaking inside, happy and nervous all at once. To this day I still feel some of that excitement whenever I flip on my computer terminal to compose a story.

After finishing my scripts and recording them for the final tape, I headed for editing, where I pieced my stories together. The editing equipment had seen better days, and always worked more efficiently after thumping on it repeatedly and giving it a good scolding, in words not printable here.

Once my pieces were "in the can," it was back to the newsroom to help produce the show. This entailed collecting and timing the scripts, then spreading them out across the floor in order of importance, until we had enough to fill the half-hour newscast. After making a quick call to the national weather service for current temperatures, it was showtime. More often than not, I literally had to sprint to the studio to reach my seat before the big hand hit 12 and the opening credits hit the airwaves. These mad dashes to the set prompted dozens of viewers to call each night and complain that my face looked shiny and my hair was a mess.

Until an additional person was hired, my job description also included doing the eleven o'clock news. This meant rearranging and updating the early news and then taping the show at about 9 P.M. (We always crossed our fingers, hoping the town wouldn't burn down or blow up between 9 and 11.) Since the late news was the last show KTVF aired before signing off, the station manager wasn't fussy about how long it ran. As long as it filled at least nine minutes, with one commercial break, both my boss and the sponsors were happy.

What I remember most from my Fairbanks experience are the mistakes I made. There were some nights when my tongue seemed to be tied in a big fat knot, and I couldn't read the copy without repeatedly stumbling over my words. One of my most embarrassing moments happened while I was sitting on the set, putting on my makeup and waiting to tape the eleven o'clock news. Suddenly I noticed the camera's red tally light was on. "Hey!" I yelled at the top of my lungs in the direction of the control booth. "We're not on the air, are we?" It turned out we were: A master control operator had accidentally flipped the switch. Unfortunately, quite a few people were tuned in to our station that night, and it was weeks before I could go out in public without viewers asking, "Weren't you the woman who was screaming on TV?"

My biggest blunder came at end of a very hectic and seemingly endless six-day work week. The competition scooped me on a big story that happened, quite literally, on my front doorstep. Upon returning to my apartment one night after covering a Boy Scouts jamboree, I discovered police and emergency crews swarming around my building. I had to skirt the crime scene tape just to reach my front door. I was too exhausted even to question what was going on. I figured it was probably a burglary or maybe a case of domestic violence. I was wrong. As I found out the next morning—by reading the headlines and watching the *other* station's news broadcast—my next-door neighbor had been murdered in an apparent drug deal gone bad. As for me, I was found guilty of breaking one of the most important rules of journalism: "Never assume."

Although my first year was filled with mistakes, it also brought plenty of adventure. I did a series of stories with federal officials who were tracking Alaska's moose population. Periodically throughout the year, we climbed into a small, single-engine plane and spent several hours flying across Alaska's vast open spaces, through river valleys and across mountain ranges, following moose that had been fitted with monitoring devices. Occasionally we would make an impromptu stop, to check things out at ground level. The pilot would suddenly point the plane's nose downward before leveling off and perfectly lining up on a short runway that was nothing more than a dirt road, in the middle of nowhere.

I traveled to tiny villages, including Nenana, probably best known for the Nenana Ice Classic. Every year a worldwide lottery is held to guess when the ice on the Tanana River will first crack. The lucky person who comes closest to guessing the exact moment wins the pool, which may contain several thousand dollars.

My visits to Nenana and other small Alaskan villages left a sharp imprint on my memory. The people of Nenana, not unlike the rest of us, are constantly struggling to come to grips with an ever-changing world. The evidence was everywhere. Many of the town's two hundred or so residents scraped by, living off the land, fishing and hunting much the same as their ancestors had. In front of each modest cabin, fish were strung up on handmade wooden drying racks, representing the hard-earned profits of the previous year's work. Looking past the old-fashioned racks, I spotted satellite dishes, beaming down images from across the globe. Elderly Alaskans slowly shuffled up and down the town's main road, while teenagers whizzed by in flashy red ATVs. It was my first look at a common theme I would come across repeatedly as a journalist: the clash of old ideas against newfangled notions.

In June I shot the Midnight Sun Baseball Tournament, held every summer in Fairbanks. Teams from Alaska, Canada, and the Lower Forty-eight meet to play ball under the summer sun that never sets. Games begin at midnight and last as late as 5 A.M. Surprisingly, I never seemed to get tired during those long summer days, despite the fact that I got very little sleep. In the winter, it was just the opposite. The darkness made me feel constantly sluggish and sleepy, and eight hours of sleep was never enough.

I had one of my most satisfying experiences covering the World Eskimo and Indian Olympics. Every year, hundreds of native Alaskans gather to compete in ancient games passed down from their ancestors. Each individual event lasted two hours, and I used the time to try out different camera techniques and concentrate on capturing interesting and unique pictures and sounds. Later, when writing the script, I paid careful attention to integrating my words with the video images. I was proud of the story when it aired. I felt it marked the first time I had successfully blended pictures, sound, and words to tell a story, a skill all successful television journalists must master.

Perhaps the most important lesson I learned that first year came from doing a story on alcoholism, a problem that the experts say has reached epidemic proportions in several Alaskan communities. During my time in Alaska, about a dozen towns passed strict prohibition laws, virtually outlawing the sale and use of alcohol. I told the story not with statistics but by profiling a handful of families whose lives had been profoundly altered by the disease. I learned that a difficult issue, affecting countless people, is sometimes best told in stories about individuals.

I stayed in Fairbanks less than a year, leaving to take a job as a reporter and photographer in a bigger market in my home state of Washington. My position was quickly filled with another novice reporter eager to break into the business. Viewers in small markets like Fairbanks get used to seeing new faces on TV, as reporters are constantly leaving for better-paying jobs in bigger cities.

I eventually wound up at the NBC affiliate in Portland, Oregon, where I wore only one hat: that of producer. I no longer lined my scripts up on the floor; instead I produced the show with the help of sophisticated computer software. As for packing around heavy camera gear, no one in Portland ever even suggested I do such a thing.

But for all the luxury of working in a large market, I am grateful for my time in Fairbanks. Seemingly impossible deadlines don't faze me a bit, and I know, without a doubt, I can manage the heaviest of workloads. After surviving my first year in television, I'm willing to venture into just about any situation. I have recently started my own video production company. The foundation of my new business is being built on all the many skills I acquired while I was a one-man band, eighty miles south of the Arctic Circle.

Kelly Huotari is a free-lance video producer based in Seattle, Washington.

Bibliography

Block, Mervin. *Rewriting Network News: WordWatching Tips from 345 TV and Radio Scripts.* Chicago: Bonus Books, Inc., 1990.

Coates, Charles. *Professional's TV News Handbook.* Chicago: Bonus Books, Inc., 1994.

Cohen, Jeff and Norman Solomon. *Adventures in Medialand: Behind the News, Beyond the Pundits.* Monroe, Me.: Common Courage Press, 1993.

Filoreto, Carl with Lynn Setzer. *Working in T.V. News: The Insider's Guide.* Memphis, Tenn.: Mustang Publishing Co., 1993.

Kaniss, Phyllis. *Making Local News.* Chicago: University of Chicago Press, 1991.

Cohler, David Keith. *Broadcast Newswriting.* Englewood Cliffs, N.J.: Prentice Hall, 1990.

McLuhan, Marshall. *Understanding Media.* Cambridge, Mass.: MIT Press, 1994.

Mayer, Martin. *Making News.* Boston: Harvard Business School Press, 1993.

Meeske, Milan D. and R. C. Norris. *Copywriting for the Electronic Media: A Practical Guide.* Belmont, Calif.: Wadsworth Publishing Co., 1987.

Pringle, Peter K., Michael F. Starr, and William E. McCavitt. *Electronic Media Management.* Boston: Focal Press, 1995.

York, Ivor. *Basic TV Reporting.* Boston: Focal Press, 1994.

Zettle, Herbert. *Television Production Handbook.* Belmont, Calif.: Wadsworth Publishing Co., 1992.

Index

ABC, 32, 35, 40
ABC affiliates
   Boston, Massachusetts, 29, 52
   Buffalo, New York, 71–74
   Seattle, Washington, 92
ABC News, xvi, 34, 35, 54–59, 86–90
ABC Sports, 37
"About Men" column, 41
Agents, 41
Anchor(s), 4–5, 57, 74
Anchor-reporter(s), 93–100
Anchoring, 83, 84
Anderson, Terry, 58
Anna, Illinois, 21
Arnold, Roseanne, 17
Arnold, Tom, 17
Associate producer(s), 8, 20, 26, 35, 66
Awards/honors, 34, 38, 84

Barnard College, 85
Barry, Dave, 54
Barry, Marion, 59
Bay City Times, 1, 2
Breaking story(ies), 72
Briefing packet(s), 58
Broadcast journalism, degree in, 92

Buffalo, New York, 71–74
Bush, George, 88

Cable News Network (CNN), xvi, 1–10, 85
Camera operators, 24, 57, 64, 65–66
Cape Girardeau, 25–26
Capra, Frank, 16
CBS, 40
CBS affiliates
   Columbus, Georgia, 22–25
   Lincoln, Nebraska, 44–50
CBS News, 26, 31
Celebrities, 17–18, 20, 88–89
"Chorus Line, A," 56
Chyron operator(s), 23–24
CNN
   see Cable News Network (CNN)
"CNN Headline News," 26
Collaboration, 86, 90
   see also Teamwork
Columbia University, 52, 54, 55, 85
Columbus, Georgia, 22, 25, 26
Commercial breaks, 24–25
Commercials, 67
Communications degree, 8

Index

Community-access station(s), 62–63
Company Store, 81–82
Consumer advocate news, 76–77
Continuity supervision, 31
Copy aide(s), 36
Copy editing, 9
Copy editor, 5, 9
Copywriting, 26
Correspondents, 57
Cosell, Howard, 36–37, 38–40
Cover letter(s), 12, 36
Craiglow, Alison, xvi, 85–90
"Current Affair, A" (TV program), 14
Cut-ins, 83, 96

David, Larry, 41
Deadlines, xvii, 10, 86, 100
"Dear John" (TV program), 16
Deaton, Robert, 66–67
Desk assistant(s), 54, 55, 57, 86–89
Desk assistant job(s), 92
  competition for, 90
Detroit, Michigan, 74, 76–77
Diamond, Ed, 31
Director(s), 5, 24–25
Discovery, 35
Documentaries, 32–33, 34–35, 67, 84
Donaldson, Sam, 88–89
Dukakis, Michael, 28–29, 88

Editing, 74, 80, 83, 97
  video, 26, 62–63, 65
Editors, 57
  unionized, 65
Educational background, 8, 28, 42, 43, 52–53, 60–61, 69, 71, 76, 84, 85, 91
  prerequisite to television journalism, 92
Emmys, 34, 38, 84
Emotions
  in/and news, 73–74
Employment
  experience and, xvi, 62, 92
  market size and, 22, 74, 78, 83–84

Entertainment Weekly, 16
Entry-level jobs, xvi, 34, 35, 69–71, 91
  learning required in, 23, 26, 37, 47–49, 53–54, 55–56, 63, 65, 71, 79–80, 86–89, 92–93, 100, 101
  work performed in, 55–56
Executive producer(s), 47
Experience
  and employment, xvi, 62, 92
  importance of, 44
  pre-professional, 21–22, 28, 42–44, 52–53, 60–62, 85, 86–87
Extras, 60

Faber, Laura, xvi, 76–84
Fact checking, 34, 57–59
Fairbanks, Alaska, 91, 93–100
Fairbanks Daily News Miner, 96
Film, 60–62, 64–65, 66–67, 68
First years, xv, 67, 68
Flanigen, George, xvi, 60–68
Floating production assistant (PA), 8–9
Fonter(s), 23
Fonts, 9, 23
Freelance associate producer(s), 35
Freelance researcher/production assistant, 31
Freelance writing, 40–41
Freelancing
  in film, 66–67
Friendly, Fred, 31
Friends as contacts, 30–31, 32, 62, 64
"Frontline" (TV program), 35

Gabor, Zsa Zsa, 4, 17
General assignment reporter(s), 1, 78, 83
General manager(s), 49–51
"Geraldo" (TV program), 17
"Good Morning America" (TV program), 16–17, 71, 76
Green Eyeshade Award, 84
Grip(s), 93

Hume, Brit, 88
Huotari, Kelly Schnell, xvi, 91–101

Index

Independent production companies, 32–34
Information developers, xi
Information superhighway, x
Initiative, 7–8
Internships, xvi, 42–43, 52–53, 54, 63, 76–77, 80
  importance of, 74–75
  print journalism, 85
Interviewing
  learning, 71
Interviews, (job), 22–23, 29, 36–37, 40, 44–45, 62, 92
  on television, 39, 75
Investigative reporting, 81–82
Iris Award, 84

"Jelly Roll Review" (TV program), 69–71
Jennings, Peter, 87
Job mobility (CNN), 9
Journalism, 37, 52–53
  see also Print journalism; Television journalism
Journalism degree, 8
Just, Sara, 52–59

"Kelly & Co." (TV program), 76
Kennedy, Bobby, 34
Kennedy, John, 34
KING-TV (Seattle, Washington), 93
KOLN (Lincoln, Nebraska), 44–50
KOMO-TV (Seattle, Washington), 92
Koppel, Ted, 58–59
KTVF (Fairbanks, Alaska), 91, 93–100

LaCrosse, Wisconsin, 78–83
Lawrence, Vicki, 20
Learning on the job, xvi, 4
  about other parts of operation, 8, 23, 24, 25, 37, 48–49, 55–56, 65, 71, 79–80, 86–89, 92–93
Line producer(s), 8
Local news, 53–54

Local organization technician(s), 65
Location scout(s), 29–31
Loyalty, 13–14
Lyons, Paula, 52

McDermott, Deb, 42–51
McMartin preschool case, 58–59
Magazine writing, 40
Margolis, Sherry, 69–75
Maris, Roger, 39
Market size, 80
  and employment, 22, 74, 78, 83–84
Markets, small, 22, 100
"Maury Povich Show" (TV program), 12–13, 14, 16, 17–20
Mehlman, Peter, 36–41
Memphis State, 61, 64
Menial work, xv, 6, 93
Mentor(s), 13–16, 20
Michigan State University, 76
Midnight Sun Baseball Tournament, 99
Mission, sense of, xvii, 27, 50–51, 89–90
Mistakes, 4–5, 39–40, 48, 57–58, 63, 74, 88, 97–98
  accepting responsibility for, 80–81
  learning from, 65
Musburger, Brent, 37
Music videos, 67

Nashville, Tennessee, 26, 49, 50–51, 79, 82, 83–84
Nashville Network, 61
NBC, 32
NBC affiliates
  Portland, Oregon, 100
  Seattle, Washington, 93
NBC-CBS affiliates
  Fairbanks, Alaska, 91, 93–100
Nelson, Cindy, xvi, 21–27
Nenana Ice Classic, 98–99
Networking, 29
New York Times, 41, 85
News, 9, 29, 57, 69, 76–77
  local, 53–54

News (*cont'd*)
  radio, 71
  television, 54, 75, 89–90, 91–92
News director(s), 24, 82–83
News packages, 3
News reporting, 77
News sense, 57
Newsmagazine shows, 90
Newspaper experience
  college, 21, 52, 53, 69, 85, 86–87
  high school, 21, 69
Newsroom, 5, 6, 86–87
Nickelodeon, 32–33
"Nightline" (TV program), xvi, 54–59
North America Dogsled Championships, 94–95

Oakland Raiders, 38
On-camera presence, 71–72
On-camera skills, learning, xvi
On-the-job training, 24, 92
  see also Learning on the job

Passion for one's work, 50, 51
Patriot Ledger, The, 53–54
Patti, Sandi, 67
Pay-TV, 38
PBS, 32
  Boston affiliate, 29–31
Peer support, 80
People management, 43, 48, 50
Persian Gulf War, 9
Political reporting, 28–29
Portfolio(s), 12, 45
Portland, Oregon, 100
Povich, Maury, 12–13, 14, 15, 16, 19
Preinterviews, 39
Preproduction, 23–24
Pre-professional experience, 21–22, 28, 42–44, 52–53, 60–62, 85, 86–87
Press releases, 45, 47, 48
Print journalism, 2, 54, 85, 86, 89
  academic preparation for, 42
  television differs from, 90

Producer(s), 5, 9, 26, 57, 66, 100
  associate, 8, 20, 26, 35, 66
  executive, 47
  freelance, 29, 30
  independent, xi
  line, 8
Producing, 83
Production, 34, 62, 63, 97
  learning, 71
  of television news, 93
Production assistant, 32, 33
  floating, 8–9
  freelance, 31
Production associate(s), 89
Production companies
  independent, 32–34
  video, 100–101
Program suppliers, xi
Promotion(s), 24, 66, 89
  CNN, 4, 6, 7
  denied, 82–83
Public relations, 42, 43, 44, 47, 77
Public TV, 31
Publicists, 16, 20

Radio news, 71
Radio work, 21, 22, 23, 71, 72
  pre-professional, 21, 28, 42
  value of experience in, 74
Ratings, 19, 89
Raw logging, 6–7
Rejection letters, 53, 62
Relocating, 13
Reporter(s), 74, 75
  general assignment, 1, 78, 83
  town, 53–54
Reporting
  emotions in/and, 73–74
  investigative, 81–82
  live, on-camera, 79–80
  political, 28–29
Research, 34, 57–59
Résumé(s), 22, 53, 61–62, 63–64, 75, 77–78

Index

Résumé tape(s), 22, 77–78, 80, 92, 93
Reynolds, Burt, 60
Reynolds, Debbie, 17
Rochester, Minnesota, 83, 84

Salaries, 7, 9, 26–27, 33–34, 86, 94
"Sally Jessy Raphael" show, 12
Scene III (production house), 61
Scott, Charlotte, 76, 77
Script ripper(s), 3, 4–5, 6, 7, 9
Script writing, 39, 40–41
Scripts
  writing, recording, 96–97, 100
Seiken, Jason, 53
"Seinfeld" (TV program), 41
Shooting, 74, 83, 88
  on location, 39
Sitcoms, 41
Skills learning, 23, 24, 25, 26, 48–49, 100, 101
  entry-level jobs, 71
  pre-professional, 87
South Dakota State University, 42
Southern Illinois University, Carbondale, 21
Special projects, 66
Spectator, The (newspaper), 53, 85
Sports journalism, 37–38, 39–40
"SportsBeat" (TV program), 36–40
Staff
  helping new people, 47, 53
State University of New York at Buffalo, 71
Stern, David, 38
Supers, 9

Tabloids, 14, 17
Talent booker/coordinator(s), 12–20
Talent executives, 13–16
Talk shows, 17, 20
Tape logger(s), 6–7, 9
Tape operators, 24–25
Teamwork, xvii, 57, 65
  see also Collaboration

Technical aspects/staff, 2–3, 5, 24, 49, 72
Telecommunications, x–xi, 76
Telecommunications degree, 8
Teleprompter, 3, 4, 5, 24, 50, 56–57
Television, xi–xii, 2, 9
  entry into, 11–12
  as medium, 31
  working in, xvi–xvii, 89, 90
Television journalism, 2
Television news, 54, 75, 89–90, 91–92
Television reporting
  difference from radio, 71–72
Television stations
  pre-professional experience at, 21–22
Terminology (television), 56
Time magazine, 53, 54
Tony Franco (PR firm), 77, 78
Town reporter(s), 53–54
Training on the job
  see Learning on the job; On-the-job training
"20/20" (TV program), 35

Union regulations, 65, 74, 76, 80
University of Southern California, 31
"Up to the Minute" (TV program), 26

Viacom Cablevision, 62, 65
Video, xi, 49
  selecting for news briefs, 87–88
Video editor(s), 32
Video editing, 26, 62–63, 65
Video experience, 62–63
Video journalist (VJ) program (CNN), 1–2, 4–6, 8–9
Video production company(ies), 100–101
Videotape library(ies), short–term, 6, 7
Vineys, Kevin, xvi, 1–10

Walker, Jason, 11–20
Walker, Mia Freund, xvi, 28–35
Walters, Barbara, 35

Washington Post, 36, 37
WBZ (Boston), 29
WCBV (Boston), 52
Weather reporting, 25, 78–83
Western Airlines, 42–43, 46
WGBH (Boston), 29–31
William Morris (agency), 14
"Wonder Years, The"
   script for, 40–41
World Eskimo and Indian Olympics, 99–100

"World News Tonight" (TV program), 89
WRBL-TV (Columbus, Georgia), 22–25
Writers, 5, 9
Writing, 69, 74, 86
   freelance, 40–41
   script, 39, 40–41
WXYZ-TV Channel 7 (Detroit), 76–77

"Young and the Restless, The" (TV program), 16